DISNEY'S

WONDERFUL WORLD OF KNOWLEDGE

Myths and Legends

Disney's
Wonderful
World of
Knowledge

THE DANBURY PRESS

THE DANBURY PRESS

a division of Grolier Enterprises, Inc.

ROBERT B. CLARKE   *Publisher*

ARNOLDO MONDADORI EDITORE

MARIO GENTILINI   *Editor-in-Chief*

ELISA PENNA   *Supervising Editor*

GIOVAN BATTISTA CARPI   *Illustrators*
CLAUDIO MAZZOLI

GUIDO MARTINA   *Author*

CONTENTS

THE GREAT MYTHS OF LONG AGO

At last, boys and girls, my great moment has come. In case you do not already know it, my name is Minnie—Minnie Mouse—and I have been chosen to be your personal guide through the land of myths and legends.

I should really begin by telling you what myths and legends are and why they have been important to all of the peoples of the world. Myths and legends are really very much alike. If there is a difference between them, myths are more likely to explain the natural world of man through the adventures of gods and goddesses. There are, for instance, myths to tell why the wind blows and why man has the wonderful tool of fire. Legends, on the other hand, are stories that explain a people's history through the adventures of great heroes and heroines.

You will find both myths and legends in this book. I hope you find them as interesting and exciting as I do.

I think it would be a good idea to begin at the beginning—I mean at the very beginning of time. It seems only right to start with the story of the beginning of the world as the ancient Greeks told it. Many of the myths and legends that we are most familiar with are based on the myths and legends of ancient Greece, or the Roman versions of them.

The people of ancient Greece had a name for the condition of the earth when it was brand new and still unformed. They called this condition Chaos. We still use the word "chaos" to mean a state of great confusion. The ancient gods emerged from Chaos to give the young earth order and form. One of the first gods to emerge was Gaea, the goddess or mother of the earth. Gaea gave birth to many other gods and goddesses. It was her huge family that came to rule on Mount Olympus, the highest mountain in Greece, where the gods were said to live. Gaea's descendants were the most powerful of the ancient gods, honored both by the Greeks and by the Romans. They included Hera (queen of the gods, whom the Romans called Juno), Zeus (the powerful king of the gods, whom the Romans called Jupiter or Jove), Ares (Mars), Poseidon (Neptune), and many others.

You must not think that because these gods and goddesses were heavenly beings everything went smoothly for them. They were often short-tempered, quarrelsome (with one another and with mortals), and changeable. As a matter of fact, nothing ever went smoothly for them! That is probably why there are so many good stories to tell about them.

9

THE GIFT OF FIRE

And man? When did man make his first appearance on earth? Greek mythology gives us some fascinating answers to this very basic question. And a remarkable being named Prometheus emerges as man's first friend and champion.

Prometheus was a demigod (a being with more power than a mortal but less than a god). Because of his interest in the human race, Prometheus was champion of mankind from the very beginning. And from the beginning men had trouble with the gods.

Mythology tells us a number of stories about how man came to be. The two most famous involve Prometheus. In one version we are told that all men are descended from Pelasgus, who had sprung from the rich soil of the Arcadia region of Greece. At first the children of Pelasgus were perfect, living happily together. However, in the second generation the grandchildren of Pelasgus came to know hatred and evil, and they quarreled among themselves. They were no longer perfect.

Zeus, the father of the gods, was angry and disappointed with mankind. He im-

10

posed the worst penalty he could think of on the human race. He was not going to give them a most important tool—fire! Prometheus felt very sorry for his human friends, for fire was necessary for light and heat and cooking—and thousands of other things. Prometheus decided to defy Zeus. He stole a lightning bolt from the heavens and with it gave fire to man.

Zeus was furious. He had the powerful demigod chained to a rock and exposed to raging storms and burning sun. To increase his suffering he sent a great eagle to the rock daily to tear at the liver of the helpless demigod. Some versions of the myth say that Prometheus was held captive for 1,000 years.

Another version of the myth gives Prometheus an even more important role in man's history. This version says that Prometheus made the first man himself—actually molding him out of clay he scooped up from the ground. The goddess Pallas Athene (whom the Romans called Minerva) then gave the newly formed creature some interesting traits. Among these traits were the strength of the lion, the pride of the peacock, the shrewdness of the fox, and the shyness of the hare.

Opposite page: Prometheus chained to a rock as punishment for his kind deeds.
Above: Bas-relief shows the powerful family of gods ruled by Zeus.

The rest of this version of the myth is the same. Zeus was dissatisfied with man as Prometheus made him and withheld fire. And, of course, Prometheus gave fire to his people and was punished.

Which of these stories do you like best? Take your choice. But now let's get on to a very important matter—the adventures of the first woman.

PANDORA'S BOX

She was beautiful, wise, talented, charming, learned, elegant, light, and graceful. When the first woman, Pandora, appeared, she seemed the most perfect and delightful of creatures. Zeus himself was said to have ordered her creation. But you know from the other stories I have told you that Zeus was not an easy god. The truth is that lovely Pandora was another of his tricks on mankind.

One version of the myth tells us that Zeus was still determined to punish man in some way. Prometheus had ruined everything by giving fire to man, so Zeus had to think of something new. He knew that Prometheus had locked all of the evils that might befall mankind in a box and sealed it. This gave Zeus an idea. He offered the beautiful Pandora to Epimetheus, the brother of Prometheus, as a bride. He sent the dangerous, sealed box with her, saying it was a fine treasure and would be her dowry.

Prometheus had warned his brother against accepting gifts of any kind from Zeus. But poor Epimetheus was so overwhelmed by the beauty of Pandora that he forgot his brother's advice and married her.

Pandora had been warned not to open the mysterious box. But she was a woman and naturally curious. (Mickey says I'm a little nosy, too.) One day she could

resist the temptation no longer and opened the box. Out flew all of the evils that were to afflict mankind—disease, war, sorrow, death, and many others. Neither the heartbroken Pandora, Epimetheus, nor Prometheus could put the evils back.

But there was one happy note in the story. One thing is said to have remained in the box: Hope. And it has always been hope that has made mankind able to bear its worst problems.

FROM ZEUS TO THE FLOOD

Zeus was horrified when he saw the terrible things that happened to man after Pandora opened the awful sealed box. As he looked down at earth from Mount Olympus, he saw thefts, fights, riots, wars,

pickpockets at work, murder, and many other disasters. He was determined to teach the human race a lesson. He caused a great flood to completely cover the earth. Everyone was drowned except for two lucky people. They were King Deucalion, who was called the most honest man on earth, and his wife Pyrrha. As you might imagine, it was not Zeus who saved these two. It was an old friend, Prometheus.

Pyrrha and Deucalion were children of beings whom you already know about. Deucalion was the son of Prometheus. Pyrrha was the daughter of Epimetheus and his unlucky wife Pandora. Prometheus heard what Zeus had in store for the human race and he warned Deucalion and Pyrrha. He told them to build a boat so that they could save themselves and so save humanity.

When the floor came, the royal couple sailed off on their boat. They sailed for 9 days and 9 nights. On the 10th day the water receded. They found themselves —and their boat—perched on top of Mount Parnassus, a sacred mountain that was one of the tallest peaks in Greece.

Deucalion and Pyrrha had been told that they must—as soon as the waters receded—"throw the bones of the Great Mother over their shoulders." Deucalion was wise as well as good. He knew that since the earth was the Great Mother of humans, her bones must be stones. Deucalion threw stones over his shoulder and miraculously they became men. Pyrrha did the same and her stones became women.

And so the human race had a new start. Their friend Prometheus had launched them on the long road to civilization.

13

Snowy peaked Mount Parnassus in
Greece was sacred to the ancient
gods. A modern shepherd tends
his flock, and the old magic is still
in the air.

THE SUN CHARIOT

Mythology also tried to explain to man the movements of the sun and the moon, the stars and the planets.

In Greek mythology Helios was the Sun god. He was the brother of Selene (the Moon) and of Eos (the Dawn). He was a splendid, glowing fellow with shining eyes, curly, golden hair, and a gold helmet.

Every morning when Helios woke in his palace in Ethiopia, Eos would swing open the palace gates and the Hours, who were his servants, would harness four prancing horses to his chariot. The chariot had golden wheels with silver spokes. The radiant Sun god would then begin his dazzling journey across the sky. In the evening he would return to his palace.

Helios had a lovely wife and a fine son. She was Clymene, the daughter of Oceanus (the Ocean god). His son was Phaethon—a name meaning "brilliant."

Naturally young Phaethon was very proud of his handsome and famous father. He liked to brag about him to his friends.

He bragged so much that his friends began to say they did not believe a word of the stories he told about the splendid, shining Sun chariot his father drove. Phaethon grew so angry at their teasing that he went much too far one day and said his father was going to let him, Phaethon, drive the Sun chariot.

That night Phaethon begged his father to let him drive the next day. After much pleading, Helios said yes. The next morning the eager boy mounted the chariot and took the reins. The horses knew at once that an amateur was trying to drive them. They galloped wildly away, shaking the reins from Phaethon's hands. They jumped high in the sky and burned a white furrow, or path, which some myths say is the Milky Way. Then the horses galloped much too close to earth and burned great areas of land and dried up oceans and rivers with the great heat of the Sun chariot. Thus, the deserts were formed, the myths say.

Zeus saw all this damage and could not allow poor Phaethon to continue his destructive ride. He struck the runaway chariot down with a thunderbolt.

Below: A Viking sculpture of the chariot of the Sun.
Right: An ancient Greek vase painting shows Helios in the Sun chariot driving his team of winged horses.

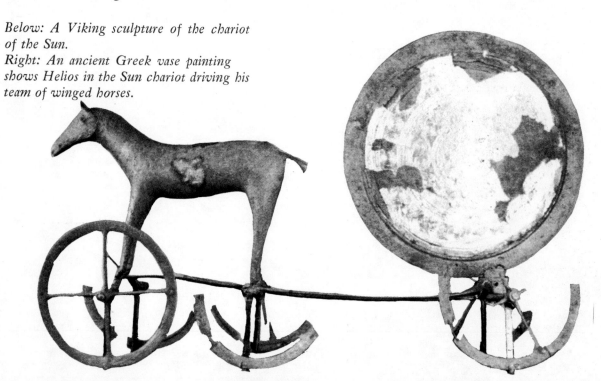

The exciting Renaissance drawing above shows the moment at which the unlucky Phaethon toppled from the swift chariot of the Sun. The myth says that the unfortunate boy fell into the Po River in Italy, while his horrified sisters the Heliades watched. The Heliades were so sad at their young brother's fate and wept so much that Zeus changed them into poplars. Poplars, growing on the banks of the Po, are seen in the background of the photograph at right. It is said that the wind blowing through the poplars along the river still carries the sound of the Heliades weeping.

TANTALUS

Now we come to another strange myth. This one is about a king named Tantalus. Tantalus had everything: power, riches, the love of his people, and—most important of all—the love of the gods. But he wanted even more. Since he had all earthly power and riches, he began to grow jealous of the divine power of the gods. He grew eager to know all their secrets.

The one thing Tantalus wanted most to learn was whether or not the gods were all-knowing. To find out, he invited them to a banquet. For the main course, he had his own son Pelops made into a stew. If the gods were all-knowing, the crafty Tantalus thought, they would refuse to eat the stew. If they were not and did eat it, then he could blackmail them until they gave him, Tantalus, everything he wanted.

The trick failed. The gods knew at once what Tantalus had done and they brought poor Pelops back to life. They condemned Tantalus to be eternally punished for his wickedness. One punishment was to have a tree with beautiful fruit growing near him, but whenever he reached out to pick the fruit, the branches would move from his grasp. The word "tantalize," which is based on the king's name, describes the feeling we have when something we want is just out of reach.

NIOBE

King Tantalus, the odd fellow in the last myth, also had a daughter. Her name was Niobe and she was like her father.

Married to King Amphion of Thebes, Niobe was haughty and ambitious. She had 14 beautiful children—seven boys

19

and seven girls. Niobe was so pleased with herself that she dared make fun of the goddess Leto, who was honored by the women of Thebes. Leto had two children, Apollo and Artemis. Niobe boasted that she was worthier of honor than Leto since she had so many more children than the goddess.

Leto became furious. One day when Niobe's sons and daughters were outdoors, they were shot by invisible arrows. Apollo and Artemis had avenged their mother.

Niobe wandered through Greece mourning her children. When she came to Mount Sipylus, Zeus changed her into a marble statue. The statue's face remained wet with tears.

THE GREAT HEROES

Of all the exciting stories that we have inherited from the people of ancient Greece and Rome, my favorite stories are those told about men called "heroes." We still use the word "hero" to describe a man who performs brave or gallant deeds —like Mickey, every once in a while. However, the people of the ancient world meant something special when they spoke of heroes.

In order to understand heroes, it might help if we remembered some of the unusual beings we have already discussed. First of all, the ancient world believed that the gods ruled over the world of lesser beings. Lesser beings meant not only man

Opposite page: The awful face of the Gorgon Medusa as it might have appeared reflected in the shield of Perseus—snaky hair and all. Below: The statue of Perseus shows the handsome young hero holding aloft the magical head of Medusa, after cutting it from her writhing body.

and the animals but demigods, nymphs, heroes, and many other creatures. The gods were immortal and all-powerful, even though many of them had some human characteristics. We have already discussed demigods—remember Prometheus?

But heroes were a very special breed. They were basically human. Some had been immortal but had become human. Others had almost godlike strength or a gift that placed them above average men. All of them had fascinating adventures with both gods and men.

One of the most famous of all the heroes was named Perseus. Many of the strange things that happened to him were decided before he was born.

Before Perseus was born his grand-

The ruins of Mycenae (opposite page) where Agamemnon, Menelaus, and many other heroes of Homer's Odyssey lived. At a bare, strange spot like this (above), deep in the North African desert, the ancients believed you could find the enchanted Garden of the Hesperides. Some walls of the fabled city of Tyre (above, right) still stand.

father Acrisius, king of Argos, went to an oracle (a person who could foretell the future). The oracle said that Acrisius would be killed by one of his own grandchildren. When the king's daughter Danae gave birth to a fine son whom she called Perseus, the king was frantic. He did not dare kill the child for fear the gods would punish him. Instead he locked his daughter and the child in a large chest and had the chest thrown into the sea. Fortunately for our story, the chest floated and was washed ashore on an island called Seriphus. There the young mother and her child were given shelter by a kind fisherman named Dictys. Perseus was raised by the fisherman as his own son.

Dictys had a powerful brother named Polydectes, who was king of the island. Polydectes wanted to marry Danae but she refused. The king was bitter and resented Danae and her son Perseus, who was now almost grown. The king announced his marriage to another woman and commanded that each of his subjects give him a horse as a wedding gift. Because he was poor and very brave, Perseus said he could not give a horse but he would bring the king another present—the head of the fierce Gorgon named Medusa.

Medusa was terrifying. She was one of three strange sisters called Gorgons. She had once been a beautiful young woman but she had insulted the powerful goddess Athena. Athena changed her into a hideous monster. Her hair became a mass of writhing serpents. Her face became so terrible that any human who looked directly at her was turned to stone.

Polydectes thought he had seen the last of Perseus. But Perseus was no ordinary young man. The gods were willing to help him. Athena gave him a brightly polished shield. Hermes gave him an unbreakable

24

sickle (a curved steel blade).

With the help of the gods Perseus found the cave where Medusa and her sister Gorgons lived. Medusa was the only one of them who could be killed. Perseus advanced on Medusa, careful to look only at her reflection in his shield. He cut off her head with one stroke of the sickle Hermes had given him. As the blood from Medusa's body fell to the ground, it caused the famous winged horse Pegasus to spring from the soil.

Perseus returned eventually to Seriphus and showed the astonished Polydectes his magical trophy. The king was so frightened at Perseus' strength and bravery that he agreed to leave him and his mother alone. Perseus went off to new adventures.

But the best is yet to come. Wait until you hear what happened when Perseus had to save a beautiful young maiden from a terrible monster.

An ancient statue of the mythical winged horse Pegasus, which Perseus brought to life when he killed the Medusa.

THE BEAUTIFUL ANDROMEDA

Andromeda was the daughter of Cepheus, an Ethiopian king, and his wife Cassiopeia. Andromeda was very beautiful. In fact, her mother boasted that Andromeda was the most beautiful child ever born—more beautiful than the lovely Nereids, the daughters of Poseidon, the sea god.

That made Poseidon furious. He flooded Ethiopia. Then he sent a huge sea serpent to devour the population. The people were scared to death. They asked their gods what would save them. The only answer, they were told, was to sacrifice Andromeda to the monster. Sadly, Cepheus had his daughter chained to a cliff at the edge of the sea.

Perseus saw the lovely girl in distress. He fell in love at first sight. He told Cepheus that he would slay the monster if he could marry Andromeda. The king agreed and Perseus proceeded to cut off the monster's head with his magic sickle. Perseus claimed Andromeda as his bride.

THE PROPHESY COMES TRUE

Perseus and Andromeda were very happy. After their wedding festivities were over, they went back to Argos where Perseus had started his amazing journey. He wanted to find his grandfather and make up with him. Acrisius, however, was frightened. He remembered the prophesy too well: that he would be

The statue (opposite page) shows the Egyptian god Amon-Re (or Ammon, as the Greeks and Romans called him) protecting one of his followers between his front hooves. Ammon was the Egyptian god of creation and the lord of the universe. He was always shown with the head of a ram. Naturally the Greeks believed he was Zeus in disguise (a god in ram's clothing), since no one but Zeus could be so powerful. The ancient carving (above) shows one of the ferocious woman warriors called Amazons defeating a man in battle.

killed by his own grandson.

When he heard that Perseus was coming back to Argos, Acrisius fled to a place called Larissa. When Perseus heard where his grandfather had gone, he followed him there, hoping to see him. While he was in Larissa, Perseus, who was strong as well as brave, entered an athletic contest. While the discus-throwing event was in progress, Perseus stepped up to take a turn. The discus he threw was caught by the wind and hit an old gentleman in the crowd on the head, killing him. You guessed it—the old gentleman was Acrisius. Without meaning to, Perseus had fulfilled the prophesy and killed his grandfather. That was sad, wasn't it?

Perseus and Andromeda did not go back to Argos. They founded their own kingdom and raised a fine family.

A terra-cotta relief features the Corinthian hero Bellerophon on his horse, Pegasus. Bellerophon was ordered by King Iobates of Lycia to kill the Chimera, a fire-breathing, three-headed monster that was terrorizing the kingdom of Lycia. Bellerophon was Corinth's greatest hero. He enjoyed many adventures and triumphs during his early life, but he spent his later years wandering the earth in search of peace and happiness.

BELLEROPHON

I'm always surprised, boys and girls, how one myth says one thing, and another myth says something entirely different. I suppose it depends on who's telling the story. For example, some myths tell us that King Proetus had been killed by Perseus. But in the myth I'm going to tell you now, Proetus is very much alive and sitting on the throne of the kingdom of Tiryns.

Our young hero in this story was at

one time called Hipponous. However, he was given the name Bellerophon after he had killed his brother, Bellerus, during a hunt. (Bellerophon means "killer of Bellerus.") To atone for his sin, Bellerophon ran away from his home in Corinth, and made his way to the palace of Proetus, the king of Tiryns.

Proetus welcomed the traveler into his home. It was not long before Proetus' wife, Stheneboea, fell in love with young Bellerophon. Bellerophon, however, was not interested in the queen. Stheneboea became angry when her attentions were spurned and told her husband that their guest had tried to make love to her. Proetus was furious and thought up a way to send Bellerophon to his death.

Proetus asked Bellerophon to deliver a sealed message to Iobates, king of Lycia. The letter, written in code, instructed Iobates to kill the bearer of the message. Not wishing to commit the murder himself, Iobates imposed many dangerous tasks upon the young man. He hoped that Bellerophon would perish while trying to accomplish these deeds.

First, Iobates ordered Bellerophon to kill the Chimera, a great fire-breathing monster with the chest and head of a lion, the body of a goat, and the tail of a dragon. This evil monster was as fast as lightning, and its flaming breath turned all who approached it into ashes!

Bellerophon, however, had a marvelous winged horse called Pegasus. Sitting on his faithful steed, Bellerophon flew high above the earth in search of the Chimera. 29

At last he spotted the monster. Diving quickly so the Chimera would not see him, Bellerophon killed the three-headed monster by hurling a lance into its mouth.

Bellerophon next triumphed over the proud and fierce female warriors, the Amazons. On his return to Lycia, our hero safely avoided an ambush that Iobates had set for him. Iobates was so filled with admiration for Bellerophon that he gave

A bronze statue of the Chimera. The forepart of the body of this ferocious three-headed monster is a combination of a lion and goat, while the tail has the appearance of a dragon, or serpent.

his daughter in marriage to the young hero.

Years later Bellerophon, on his winged horse, Pegasus, attempted to reach the summit of Mount Olympus, home of the gods. However, Bellerophon was thrown from his horse by Zeus, the king of the gods. Lamed by the fall, poor Bellerophon roamed the earth for the rest of his life, a lonely and unhappy mortal.

31

THE LABORS OF HERCULES

Of all the heroes in Greek mythology perhaps the most familiar is Hercules, who is also known by his Greek name, Heracles. There have been so many stories about this mighty hero, boys and girls, that I feel you probably know a good deal about him. But I'm sure you would never forgive your old friend Minnie Mouse if I didn't take this opportunity to give you my version of the story of Hercules —particularly his Twelve Labors.

Zeus, the king of the gods, wished to have an earthly son who would be a very good friend to both mortals and immortals. So he had a child by Alcmene, a granddaughter of Perseus. Zeus gave the boy the name of Heracles, which means "glory of Hera." However, Hera, who was Zeus' wife and the queen of heaven, hated the child because the boy was not her own. Hera declared that she would not rest until she had her revenge. When she learned that Hercules was to become king of Mycenae when he reached manhood, Hera became furious and used her influence to secure the throne for her cousin, Eurystheus.

Hera was so jealous of Hercules that one night, while everyone was asleep, she sent two great serpents into the nursery to attack the infant. The child awoke just in time. Fearlessly, Hercules grabbed each of the monsters and strangled them with his bare fists! It's no wonder that from that day on, Hercules was regarded by everyone as a great hero.

As Hercules grew up he was carefully educated in the arts of war, boxing, and wrestling. He became expert in the use of the bow and arrow and many other weapons. Hercules had the best teachers in school. Rhadamanthus, who was also a son of Zeus, taught him wisdom, and Linus, the inventor of rhythm and melody, tutored Hercules in music. Linus insisted that his gifted student learn to play the lyre, a stringed harplike musical instrument. One day Hercules became so annoyed with Linus that he struck his teacher with the lyre. The blow was

delivered with such great force that Linus was killed instantly.

As punishment for his crime, Hercules was sent to live in the mountains in the care of shepherds. During this period he devoted a good deal of time to physical exercise and developing his strength. When he was 18 years old, Hercules performed one of many great feats. Using his tremendous strength, he killed a ferocious lion that had attacked the herd of sheep he was tending.

Shortly after this incident, Hercules was given permission to return to his home at Thebes. He arrived just in time to save the city from an enemy attack. Because of the remarkable courage that Hercules showed during the fierce battle, King Creon of Thebes gave him his daughter,

Megara, for his wife. They had two daughters, but the marriage was an unhappy one.

During all of this time the wrath of Hera hung over Hercules. One day she put him under a spell of madness, and Hercules killed his wife and children. After committing this horrible crime, Hercules prayed to the Oracle of Delphi for guidance and forgiveness. To purify himself, he was commanded to become the slave of King Eurystheus of Mycenae. It was Eurystheus who thought up the Twelve Labors of Hercules. These difficult tasks would have been impossible for any ordinary man. Why, just thinking about them makes me tired! If you turn the page, boys and girls, you'll see what I'm talking about.

1. The Nemean lion was a fearful beast that caused great destruction throughout the land of Nemea. All attempts to kill it failed because the lion had a skin that could not be pierced by arrows. Hercules lured the lion into a trap, grasped the beast with his strong arms, and strangled it. Hercules used the lion's skin as a garment and wore the head of the beast as a helmet.

2. The Lernaean Hydra was an enormous serpent with nine heads, one of which was immortal. Anyone who approached the Hydra's den in the swamps of Lerna was killed by the monster's poisonous breath. Hercules forced the monster to emerge from the marshes and tried to cut off all nine heads with his mighty club. With the help of his servant Iolaus, Hercules burnt each severed neck with a torch and crushed and buried the last immortal head.

3. The wild boar of Erymanthus was a gigantic animal that roamed the fields near Mount Erymanthus. Hercules was ordered to bring the boar back to King Eurystheus alive. To accomplish this task Hercules chased the boar up and down the mountainside for many days until it dropped from exhaustion. He picked the animal up and carried it all the way back to Mycenae. When the savage beast was presented to the king, Eurystheus became so frightened that he ran from the palace.

4. The stag of Artemis was known for its great speed, bronze hooves, and golden horns. It ran wild over the wooded hills of Arcadia. Hercules, in an attempt to capture the deer, chased after it for a year without success. He knew that the only way he would be able to trap the swift animal was with a weapon. So he wounded the deer with an arrow, thereby making it helpless.

5. The Stymphalian birds, with beaks, claws, and feathers made of bronze, infested the forest region near Lake Stymphalis. These vicious birds would fly at great heights, dropping their sharply pointed feathers on animals and children. Hercules used a great bronze shield to cover himself, and with his poisonous arrows, shot the birds down one by one.

6. The Augean stables. Augeas, King of Elis, owned many herds of sheep, cows, and cattle. All of these animals were kept in stables that hadn't been cleaned for several years. King Eurystheus commanded Hercules to clean the stables in one day. To accomplish this task Hercules altered the courses of two nearby rivers. Soon the waters were flowing in a torrent through one door of the stables and out another door.

7. The Cretan bull, a beautiful snow-white animal, emerged from the sea one day and took refuge on the island of Crete. Shortly after its arrival, the bull went mad and caused great destruction throughout the island. Hercules was sent to Crete to capture the bull and bring it back to Mycenae. When at last he found the creature, he approached it with caution. Seizing its silvery horns, Hercules threw the bull to the ground. Once the animal had been subdued, he carried it back to King Eurystheus.

8. The girdle of Hippolyta. Eurystheus' daughter Admeta, wished to own the golden girdle of Hippolyta, queen of the Amazons. Hippolyta willingly gave the girdle to Hercules to take back to Admeta. However, Hippolyta's followers, thinking their queen was being abducted, attacked Hercules. During the battle Hippolyta was killed, but Hercules escaped with the golden girdle.

9. The cattle of Geryon. Geryon was a huge man-monster with three bodies. He owned a herd of red oxen that was kept on the island of Erythia. Hercules, at the command of King Eurystheus, had to capture the entire herd and present it to the king. To accomplish this difficult task, Hercules had to fight the monster, a shepherd, and Geryon's two-headed dog.

10. The mares (horses) of King Diomedes were fed on human flesh. Hercules, accompanied by a few volunteers, journeyed to Thrace to capture these fearsome animals. As he was leading the mares from their stable, Hercules was attacked by King Diomedes. In the battle that followed, the king was thrown to the ground and eaten by his own horses. Hercules quickly gathered up the fleeing animals.

11. The golden apples of the Hesperides. King Eurystheus next ordered Hercules to bring him the golden apples that were hidden in the garden of the Hesperides. After a journey that lasted several months, Hercules finally reached the garden. Before he could enter, however, he had to slay the dragon that was standing guard. Once inside Hercules seized the apples and later delivered them to Eurystheus, who in turn gave them to his wife. She returned them to the Hesperides.

12. The capture of Cerberus. For his final labor, Hercules had to descend into the underworld to bring back Cerberus, the three-headed dog who stood guard at Hades' gate. Hercules was granted permission to capture the beast as long as he used no weapons. With his bare hands, Hercules strangled Cerberus into unconsciousness and carried the dog off to Eurystheus.

LOST ATLANTIS

As you know, boys and girls, Minnie is one very curious mouse! For many years, (more than I care to remember), I've heard several tales about the lost continent of Atlantis. In fact, there have been so many stories that I decided the only way I would find out the truth was to do my own research. The other day, while looking through some ancient manuscripts, I discovered that the story of Atlantis indirectly involves our hero friend, Hercules.

In Greek and Phoenician mythology, Hercules is supposed to have placed two enormous rocks on either side of the Strait of Gibraltar. Later the rocks were called Calpe and Abyla—the Pillars of Hercules. The pillars were bound together by a scroll, warning sailors not to go beyond that point because it was the end of the world.

The Greek philosopher, Plato, in his writing, *Timaeus*, tells us of an ancient empire called Atlantis. It was supposedly situated in the Atlantic Ocean just beyond the Pillars of Hercules. According to Plato, Atlantis had a highly developed civilization. Because of its wealth and power, the massive armies of Atlantis often set out to conquer the lands of the Mediterranean.

On one of their conquests, they were said to have been defeated by the Athenian armies. As punishment for their attack on Greece, however, the gods sent violent earthquakes and floods against Atlantis. The island is thought to have completely disappeared in one day and one night.

There is another myth that Atlantis was ruled by Poseidon, god of the sea. The island was divided into 10 sections, each administered by one of Poseidon's sons. Zeus, king of the gods and the greatest power in the universe, became very annoyed at the way Poseidon and his sons were ruling Atlantis. Zeus decided to punish the kingdom by making it disappear in a flash of devastating earthquakes and tidal waves.

Through the centuries, scholars, archeologists, and adventurers have sought to discover traces of the famed island kingdom. They've examined Plato's writings to see if there might be some additional information as to where the island was located before tragedy struck. Some scholars, unable to find any remnants of Atlantis, think that perhaps Plato invented the entire story about the lost continent. There are others, however, who feel that Plato based his writings on earlier documents and on descriptions of voyages made by early Mediterranean sailors.

We do know from inscriptions made on the walls of Medinet Habu, an Egyptian temple constructed during the reign of Ramses III, that an invasion was carried out by people coming from a kingdom lying beyond the Pillars of Hercules. The inscription tells us that the invading armies arrived in Egypt on a fleet of ships. After a fierce battle, however, they were beaten back by the Egyptians.

Greek history tells us of an invasion of men coming from the North Sea. Could these be the same people described by the Egyptians? Perhaps one day we'll know for certain. Some historians say that the lost kingdom of Atlantis is located in the depths of the North Sea, just off the coast of West Germany. Other historians believe that Odysseus' voyage, as described by the Greek poet Homer in his epic poem, the *Odyssey*, took Odysseus beyond the Pillars of Hercules and, in fact—to Atlantis!

Of course, my friends, with all of these fascinating stories, we've yet to find out if the island of Atlantis ever really did exist. I'm sure we can all agree that if traces of the lost civilization are ever found, the details of one of our most interesting—and mysterious—myths will be revealed to a large and curious audience.

THE SHIRT OF NESSUS

During one of the many adventures of Hercules, he married Deianira, the daughter of Oeneus, king of the Aetolians. One day Nessus, the centaur (half man, half horse), because of his love for Deianira, tried to kidnap her. Hercules discovered the plan and shot Nessus with a poisoned arrow. As Nessus lay dying, he gave his blood to Deianira. He told her

Calpe and Abyla, the two rocks that form the Strait of Gibraltar. These two rocks were called the Pillars of Hercules in Greek mythology.

that the blood was sacred and would act as a charm, preserving her husband's love for her.

Later Hercules challenged King Eurytus to a battle. After killing Eurytus, Hercules proclaimed his love for the king's daughter, Iole. When Deianira was informed of her husband's unfaithfulness, she remembered the words of Nessus, the centaur. She soaked a tunic in the centaur's blood and sent the cloth to Hercules, hoping to regain his love. As soon as Hercules put on the tunic, he felt himself being devoured by inner fire. Crazed with pain, he tore trees from the ground and built himself a funeral pyre. Placing himself on top of the pyre, he implored his companions to set fire to the wood. As the flames rose, a thunderous bolt of lightning filled the sky. A chariot driven by the goddess Athena appeared. She carried Hercules to Mount Olympus, where he would live as an immortal among the other gods and goddesses.

THE HERO THESEUS

One of my favorite myths concerns Theseus, a cousin of our good friend, Hercules. It's an exciting story, boys and girls, that I think you'll like.

Theseus was the son of Aethra and Aegeus, the king of Athens. Theseus was not born in Athens, but his father left orders that the child was to come to that city once he was able to perform a certain task. Shortly before King Aegeus returned to Athens, he had placed his sword and sandals under an enormous rock. Aegeus decreed that when Theseus had grown strong enough, he was to lift the rock and bring the sword and sandals to him in Athens.

Theseus spent his childhood in Troezen with his mother. When he became 16 years old, Aethra led her son to the rock and told him of his father's instructions. With great ease, Theseus lifted the rock and took his father's belongings. Soon after, Theseus began his journey to Athens to present himself to his father, King Aegeus. I'm sure that Theseus had no idea of the adventures that he would encounter on his travels. If he had, he probably would have gone by sea, as his grandfather had wanted him to do, rather than by land. However, with great determination, Theseus chose the dangerous land route.

On the first day of his journey Theseus met Periphetes, a fierce savage. Periphetes always carried a club of iron, using it to kill anyone unlucky enough to cross his path. But finally he met his match. With just a few swift blows, Theseus defeated the savage and took possession of the iron club. Our hero kept the club as a souvenir of his first victory. Wasn't that a good lesson for Periphetes?

A short time later Theseus encountered Sinis, the son of Poseidon. This evil creature had a bad habit of tying travelers to the tops of pine trees. Then he'd bend the tree until the top touched the ground. Sinis would release the pine tree and as it shot forward to an upright position, the victim would fly off into the air. After a struggle Theseus captured Sinis, giving him a dose of his own medicine.

On the slopes of Megaris, Theseus met Sciron, a wicked man who forced travelers to wash his feet. When they stooped over to do as he commanded, Sciron would kick them over the cliff into the sea. Theseus, however, was too quick for Sciron. With one kick, he sent the wicked man crashing onto the rocks at the foot of the cliff.

Theseus continued on his long journey, conquering each obstacle along the way. One of his most famous adventures occurred when he came upon the giant Procrustes. Procrustes forced his victims to lie on a bed. If the unfortunate person was too long for the bed, the giant would

Above: A Cretan coin with an engraving of the Labyrinth, a building ordered constructed by King Minos of Crete to house the dreaded Minotaur.
Right: The coin was found in the ruins of this palace near the royal city of Knossos, on the island of Crete. It was near this ancient city that Theseus, using only a sword, supposedly killed the Minotaur.

cut off whatever part of the body hung over the edge. If the person was too short for the bed, Procrustes would stretch the victim's limbs until they fit it. Theseus captured Procrustes, giving him the same treatment as punishment.

It was quite a trip for Theseus, but he finally reached Athens. However, he was still not entirely safe. Medea, the new wife of King Aegeus, became jealous of Theseus and tried to poison him. The King realized what Medea was doing and stopped his son from drinking the cup of poison. Aegeus then banished his wife from Athens.

The Athenian kingdom was greatly troubled because of a tribute that they were forced to pay to King Minos of Crete. Years before, Minos had conquered Athens. He threatened to burn the city to the ground unless every year 14 youths were sent to Crete to be eaten by the Minotaur, a monster with the body of a man and the head of a bull. Theseus declared that he would not rest until he had ended this terrible practice.

Opposite page: Sheep graze among ancient ruins on a hillside on the Isthmus of Corinth.
Above: A small town on Crete, an island in the Mediterranean Sea.
Above, right: The ruins of Eleusis, a city that was a rival of ancient Athens.

43

ARIADNE'S THREAD

Theseus felt that the best way to free his fellow citizens from their forced pledge was to kill the Minotaur. So when the time came to send the 14 young people to King Minos as a sacrifice, Theseus offered to go as one of the victims. Just before the ship departed for Crete under black sails, Theseus told his father that if he were successful in destroying the Minotaur, the returning ship would carry a white sail. If he were defeated and killed in his effort, the black sail would still be flying from the mast.

When Theseus arrived in Crete, he told Minos that he was the son of Poseidon, the ruler of the sea. To test Theseus' claim, King Minos took a golden ring from his finger and threw it into the sea. He commanded Theseus to retrieve it. Theseus dived into the churning waters and returned not only with the ring but with the golden crown of Amphitrite, Poseidon's wife. This feat greatly impressed King Minos.

Shortly after his arrival at Crete, Ariadne, the daughter of Minos, fell in love with Theseus. To win his affection, Ariadne looked for ways to help Theseus in his quest to kill the Minotaur. She told him that her father had a special building constructed to hold the fierce monster. The building, called the Labyrinth, was a vast maze of corridors and passageways that turned and twisted every which way. The Minotaur was kept in the very center of the Labyrinth. Once inside, it was easy to get lost and hard—almost impossible—to find the way out. Ariadne gave Theseus a sword with which to kill the Minotaur and a huge ball of string. She instructed Theseus to tie the end of the string to the door before he entered. As he traveled through the corridors, he was to unravel

A statue of Ariadne asleep. In Greek mythology Ariadne, the daughter of King Minos, fled from Crete with Theseus. During their voyage to Athens, they stopped on the island of Naxos. While Ariadne slept, Theseus set sail for Athens, abandoning her.

45

the string. Once he killed the beast, he could find his way out by using the string as a guide.

His mission was successful. Theseus slew the beast with his sword and escaped from the Labyrinth by following the string. Theseus quickly gathered up Ariadne and the 13 young girls and boys who had traveled to Crete with him, and they set sail for Athens. On their voyage home they stopped at the island of Naxos, where Theseus abandoned Ariadne. He did this, he said, because the goddess Minerva appeared to him in a dream and commanded him to do so. Ariadne, however, was saved by the god Dionysus, who took her to Mount Olympus in a panther-drawn chariot.

In the joy of his victory over the dreaded Minotaur, Theseus forgot to change the black sail his ship was carrying. As the vessel approached the coast of Athens, King Aegeus saw it from the shore. Because the black sail was still flying from the mast, Aegeus believed that the Minotaur had devoured his son. Stunned with grief, King Aegeus threw himself into the sea.

With his father dead, Theseus became King of Athens. He was a good ruler, who gave his people wise laws and administered justice with great fairness.

Opposite page: Theseus leaves the sleeping Ariadne on the island of Naxos. Ariadne awakens just as Theseus departs for his journey to Athens.

Right: Icarus, the son of Daedalus, is shown during his flight from Crete. Disobeying his father's warning, he flew too near the sun. The heat melted the wax holding the wings' feathers together and Icarus fell into the sea.

THE WINGS OF MAN

Have you ever wished that you had wings and could fly over mountains and up into the clouds? Well, I am going to tell you about a mythical character who made his own wings and flew through the air just like a bird. His name was Daedalus and he was known throughout Greece as the greatest architect and sculptor of his time.

Daedalus had a nephew named Talus who was also clever with his hands. Fearing that Talus would one day be greater than he was, Daedalus killed him. After that Daedalus went into exile. Finally he came to Crete, the kingdom of Minos. It was Daedalus who built the Labyrinth, described in the last chapter. King Minos was happy with Daedalus' work. But when Theseus escaped from the Labyrinth, Minos suspected that Daedalus had helped him. So he imprisoned the architect and his young son Icarus.

Daedalus was determined to escape. One day, as he watched a flock of birds circling overhead, an idea came to him. He would make wings for himself and his son and fly away from the island. Gathering all the bird feathers he could find, Daedalus fastened them together with thread and wax. In this way he shaped two pairs of wings.

On the day of the flight, Daedalus attached one pair of wings to his son and warned him, "Don't fly too high or the sun will melt the wax." Then they took off, flapping their wings like birds as they soared over the sea. At first the flight went well. But then Icarus disobeyed his father and flew toward the sun. The wax melted and the feathers dropped off. Icarus struggled to stay aloft. But it was no use. He plunged into the sea and drowned. Daedalus later found his son's body and buried it. Then he continued sadly on his way to Sicily.

Above: A view of the present-day harbor and town of the island of Syros.
Opposite page: Children playing in Herakleion, the main city of Crete. The mythical Daedalus and Icarus were held captive on this island.

49

THE LEGEND OF THE GOLDEN FLEECE

Up to now I've been talking to you about the feats of individual heroes of Greek mythology. Next we turn to the adventures of a group of men. The following legend is about a band of adventurers called the Argonauts and their search for the Golden Fleece. I have already explained the difference between myths and legends, so I won't say any more about that. Mickey always tells me not to repeat myself.

But let's get on with our story. Among the ancient rulers was a king named Pelias, whose kingdom was in Thessaly. Pelias had taken the throne away from his brother Aeson, who was then forced into exile. Aeson had a son named Jason who vowed that he would one day return to Thessaly and reclaim his father's throne.

Above: A coastal region of the Black Sea. The mythical kingdom of Colchis, where the Golden Fleece was kept, was located on the banks of the Black Sea.
Opposite page: The rolling hills of Thessaly. It was from this land that Jason and the Argonauts began their adventure.

At the age of 20, Jason traveled to Thessaly to fulfill his vow. Jason was a tall and handsome man, with long blond hair. Over his shoulder he wore the skin of a leopard he had killed and he carried two spears. Along the way he lost one of his sandals, so he arrived in the kingdom of Pelias with one foot bare.

51

When King Pelias saw Jason limping in with only one sandal, he turned pale with fright. Years before a prophet had told him, "Beware the man who comes limping into your kingdom with one sandal and one foot bare." Pelias was even more troubled when Jason told him who he was and boldly announced, "I have come to claim this kingdom for I am the rightful heir to the throne."

Pelias was a sly old schemer. He did not try to kill Jason. Instead he invited Jason to his palace and entertained him with a great feast. But all the while the king was thinking of a way to get rid of the young man. Finally he thought of a plan. When he had gained the young man's confidence, Pelias told him, "You shall have the kingdom just as you wish.

But first I ask you to perform one brave deed. You must bring back the Golden Fleece."

All Greeks of that time knew the story of the sacred ram with the Golden Fleece. The gods had sent the ram, which had the power to fly, to rescue a prince and princess. Carrying the two on its back, the ram flew to Colchis, a land on the Black Sea. Along the way the princess fell into the sea, but the young prince arrived safely in Colchis. He sacrificed the magic ram to the gods and gave the Golden Fleece to the king of Colchis as a gift. Since then the prize had been kept in a sacred grove guarded by a dragon that never slept. Every Greek hero dreamed of going across the seas to bring back the Golden Fleece.

52

Just as Pelias hoped, Jason eagerly offered to attempt the task. The crafty old king laughed to himself. He was sure Jason would not survive the dangerous journey. Meanwhile, Jason sent out a call for courageous young men to join him. Many volunteered. They included Hercules, the strong man, Theseus, whom I've already told you about, and the poet Orpheus. Jason had a large ship built to carry them all across the sea. It was called *Argo* (after its builder, Argus) and the 50 men who sailed in it were called the Argonauts.

THE VOYAGE OF THE ARGO

Jason and the Argonauts had many strange adventures on their way to Colchis. On one island a crew member was dragged off by river nymphs (beautiful maidens who served the gods). Hercules went looking for the sailor and never returned. Later the Argonauts fought with the Harpies in the land of Thrace. These strange creatures had the bodies

The figure at left wearing the winged hat is Hermes, the herald and messenger of the Greek gods. Hermes is usually shown with wings on his ankles and carrying a magic wand. Hermes was also the god of sleep and dreams and is said to have had special healing powers.

and wings of birds and terribly ugly faces. When the Argonauts came upon them, they were tormenting a blind prophet named Phineus. Every time poor Phineus sat down to eat, the Harpies would swoop down, steal most of his food, and spoil the rest.

The Argonauts rescued Phineus, who repaid their kindness by warning them about the Clashing Rocks. He explained that two floating rocks the size of islands guarded the entrance to the Black Sea. They were called the Clashing Rocks because as they tossed about they would slam together like the jaws of a sea monster. Any ship caught between them would be smashed to pieces.

But Jason had a plan for getting past the rocks. When the ship drew near them, he released a dove. The bird flew between the two rocks, which snapped together with a thunderous roar. However, the dove got through, losing only a few tail feathers.

Jason kept track of the time it took for the rocks to open and close. He decided that the ship could slip through if the oarsmen rowed with all their strength. So he gave the order and everyone rowed as hard and fast as he could. The rocks started to close again. For a moment it looked as if the ship would be crushed. But with a last burst of speed, the *Argo* raced through the narrow channel as the rocks crashed close behind them.

Jason and the Argonauts finally reached the shores of Colchis. Jason went to King Aeetes and demanded the Golden Fleece. The king did not want to lose his treasure. But he said he would let Jason have it if he tamed and harnessed two fire-breathing bulls and used them to plant dragons' teeth. A crop of warriors would then spring up, and Jason would have to kill them. The task seemed impossible.

54

MEDEA THE MAGICIAN

Fortunately for Jason, King Aeetes' daughter Medea fell in love with him. Medea was a sorceress (someone with magic powers) and a priestess who served Hecate, the goddess of magic charms. She summoned Jason to a secret meeting and gave him a magic ointment to protect him from the bulls.

Jason covered his body and his weapons with the ointment. When it was time to face the bulls, he went boldly into the pasture where they were kept. King Aeetes, the Colchians, and the Argonauts breathlessly watched. The bulls snorted and pawed the ground with their bronze hooves. The fire from their nostrils scorched the grass. But Jason approached them unafraid. The magic ointment protected him from being burned. To everyone's amazement, he quickly harnessed the bulls and planted the teeth of the dragon.

Up sprang the crop of armed warriors. Jason was surrounded. The Argonauts looked on fearfully for they thought their

The ruins of a Doric temple in Corinth. It is said that on his return from Colchis, Jason stopped at Corinth to dedicate his ship to Poseidon, god of the sea. Corinth was an important port in ancient times.

leader surely would be killed. But Medea had taught him a trick. As the warriors advanced Jason flung a rock into their midst. The warriors argued about who had thrown the rock. Words were followed by blows and before long they had killed one another.

The jubilant Argonauts carried off their hero in triumph. King Aeetes was furious, for he suspected that Medea had helped Jason. But he told Jason, "You have proved yourself a true hero. Tomorrow you shall have your reward." Secretly, however, the king planned to burn Jason's ship and slaughter the Argonauts.

Medea learned of the king's scheme and warned Jason. She offered to help him steal the Golden Fleece if he would marry her and take her to Greece. Jason agreed and together they went to the secret grove. The ever-watchful dragon was there, but Medea put him under a magic spell. Then they took the treasure and sailed away.

When King Aeetes heard what had happened, he pursued them with his

55

fastest ships. To prevent the *Argo* from being caught, Medea used witchcraft to kill her own brother, who was on one of the Colchian ships. King Aeetes was so shocked by this terrible act that he ordered his ships to return to Colchis.

Returning to Thessaly, Jason offered the Golden Fleece to King Pelias. But Pelias still refused to surrender the kingdom, so Medea arranged to have him killed. Jason and Medea were then exiled to Corinth, where they married and had two children. But Jason tired of Medea after 10 years and decided to marry a young princess. In her rage Medea killed the princess and her own two children and then fled to Athens in a chariot drawn by winged dragons. Poor Jason was left without wife, children, or kingdom.

ORPHEUS IN THE UNDERWORLD

Greek mythology is filled with tragic love stories. Now that I have told you about Jason and Medea, I am going to tell another sad tale. This one is about Orpheus, the great poet and musician who sailed with Jason and the Argonauts.

After that adventure Orpheus returned to his home in Thrace. He spent his days playing his lyre and singing sweet songs. It was said that when Orpheus sang in the forest wild beasts grew tame and even the trees and rocks gathered to hear him. All of the beautiful maidens of Thrace were in love with him. But Orpheus had eyes for only one woman—Eurydice.

Orpheus courted Eurydice and a day was set for their marriage. On the wedding day Eurydice and her bridesmaids went into the fields to pick flowers for a bridal garland. A poisonous serpent lurking in the grass bit her foot and she died.

Orpheus was overcome with grief. He prayed to the gods to return his beautiful Eurydice. When the gods did not act, Orpheus decided to go down to the Underworld—the kingdom of Hades—to bring back Eurydice. No living man had ever done this and returned. But Orpheus was willing to take any risk for Eurydice.

So Orpheus made the long journey to the world of the dead. His singing charmed Charon the boatman, who carried him across the river Styx. It also soothed the three-headed monster Cerberus, guardian of Hades' kingdom. At last Orpheus arrived before King Hades himself. He begged Hades to let Eurydice return with him.

Hades was so touched by the poet's plea that he granted the request. "The spirit of Eurydice shall follow you to the living world," he told Orpheus. "But if you look back at her, she will return to my kingdom." Our story might have ended happily if Orpheus had obeyed Hades. But, as they reached the end of the journey, Orpheus looked back and Eurydice immediately disappeared. Orpheus cried out for her to return. But it was too late. She was gone forever.

Orpheus, the singer-poet of Thrace, was a favorite of the god Apollo. In this vase painting we see Orpheus singing and playing the lyre.

56

Orpheus was so much in love with Eurydice that he followed her spirit to the Underworld when she died. After failing in his attempt to bring back Eurydice, Orpheus wandered through the forests singing of his sorrow. In this painting by Picasso, Orpheus is shown being killed by a group of Bacchantes (followers of the god Bacchus).

57

An 18th-century painting showing Paris of Troy kidnapping Helen, the wife of King Menelaus of Sparta.

THE JUDGMENT OF PARIS

Some of the greatest stories of Greek mythology are built around the Trojan War. The blind poet Homer wrote about the events of the war and its aftermath in his epic poems the *Iliad* and the *Odyssey*. Other poets and playwrights also wrote about the characters of this war that ended with the capture and destruction of the city of Troy by the Greeks. Well, boys and girls, Aunt Minnie is going to explain how that war got started.

According to the legend, it began at the marriage banquet of King Pelias of Thessaly. All of the gods and goddesses from Mount Olympus had been invited —all except one. Someone forgot to send an invitation to Eris, the goddess of discord. Eris was very upset about that and she decided to get even. During the feast

58

she suddenly appeared and threw a golden apple into the middle of the banquet table. The apple was marked "For the most beautiful."

Naturally, each of the goddesses at the party thought the apple was meant for her. Hera, the wife of Zeus, grabbed the apple, while Athena and Aphrodite protested. A quarrel broke out. Each of the three goddesses claimed the apple. Finally Zeus was asked to be the judge. But Zeus did not want to get mixed up in the fight. He knew that no matter which one he chose, the other two would become his enemies.

"An impartial judge must make the decision," he said to the goddesses. "Let it be the handsomest man in the world. The judgment shall be made by Paris, the son of King Priam of Troy."

Zeus summoned Hermes, his winged messenger. He ordered Hermes to take the three goddesses to Mount Ida, where Paris lived. I should tell you that, al-

Here we see the "face that launched a thousand ships"—the beautiful Helen, for whom the young prince Paris plunged his kingdom into war. Because of Helen, the Greeks and Trojans fought for 10 years. When the fighting was over, Troy had been destroyed and most of its inhabitants killed.

Above: The famed wooden horse given by the
Greeks as a gift to the Trojans. Soldiers hidden
inside the horse opened the gates of the city so
the Greek army could capture Troy.
Below: The ruins of a temple on one of the
Aeolian islands.

60

though Paris was the son of a king, he was then living as a simple shepherd. As a baby he had been left on Mount Ida to die because his mother dreamt that his birth would cause the destruction of Troy. But a kindly shepherd had saved Paris and raised him to manhood.

Anyway, Hermes brought the three goddesses to Paris. Now you can probably imagine what happened next. Each of the goddesses played up to Paris in order to influence his decision. Hera promised him the power to rule over all men. Athena, goddess of wisdom, said he could be the wisest man in the world. And Aphrodite, goddess of love, offered him the love of the world's most beautiful woman.

Paris chose Aphrodite's gift and awarded her the golden apple. Naturally the other two goddesses were angry. They swore that someday they would take revenge. Meanwhile the years went by and Paris was reunited with his father, King Priam. The old king was so happy to see his lost son that he forgot about his wife's dream.

After awhile Paris was sent by his father on a mission to Greece. There the young prince met and fell in love with Helen, the most beautiful woman in the world. The goddess Aphrodite kept her promise. She arranged to have Helen fall in love with Paris.

Unfortunately Helen was already married to Menelaus, the king of Sparta. But Paris would not let that stand in his way. When King Menelaus went off on a jour-

An ancient Greek sibyl (prophetess) made her prophecies from this spot at Cumae, located on the Italian coast near Naples.

Left: Laocoön, the priest of Apollo, who warned the Trojans not to accept the wooden horse, is shown with his sons in the deadly coils of a serpent.

Above: Achilles and Ajax, two Greek heroes of the Trojan War, play at dice during a pause in the fighting.

63

ney to Crete, Paris kidnapped Helen and took her back to Troy.

Now when Helen had married Menelaus, Zeus had made all of the Greek princes vow to protect the couple. So all of the Greek heroes and princes gathered to join Menelaus in a war against Troy. Among those who went to fight the Trojans were King Nestor of Pylos, the great warrior Achilles, and Odysseus (Ulysses), the king of Ithaca. They set sail in a great fleet of 1,000 ships led by Agamemnon, the brother of Menelaus. After many hardships, the Greeks reached Troy. And so began the legendary Trojan War. It lasted 10 years, until the city was destroyed and Helen was taken safely back to Greece.

Opposite page: The blind poet Homer, who told of the adventures of the Greek heroes in the Trojan War. Homer is credited with writing two great poems about the war and its aftermath. The first was called the Iliad, and the second the Odyssey.

Left: A coastal village near Porto Badisco, Italy. It was here that a ship bearing Trojan survivors of the war is said to have taken refuge after the fall of Troy.

GAEA (Earth) **TARTARUS**

THE FAMILY TREE OF THE GODS

The gods worshiped by the people of ancient Greece and Rome and their near relations formed an enormous family. This chart shows the most famous members of that family and their connections with each other. The names in capital letters are the English or Greek names of the gods or other beings. The Roman names of some of the gods—or of the ideas represented by them—often appear in parenthesis beneath the Greek names.

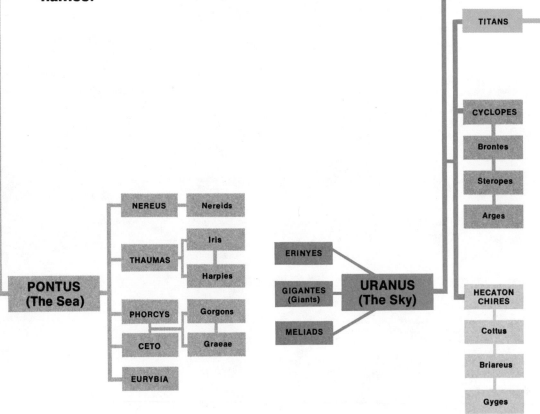

TITANS

CYCLOPES
Brontes
Steropes
Arges

NEREUS — Nereids

THAUMAS — Iris

Harpies

ERINYES

GIGANTES (Giants) URANUS (The Sky)

PONTUS (The Sea)

PHORCYS — Gorgons

MELIADS

HECATON CHIRES
Cottus

CETO — Graeae

EURYBIA

Briareus

Gyges

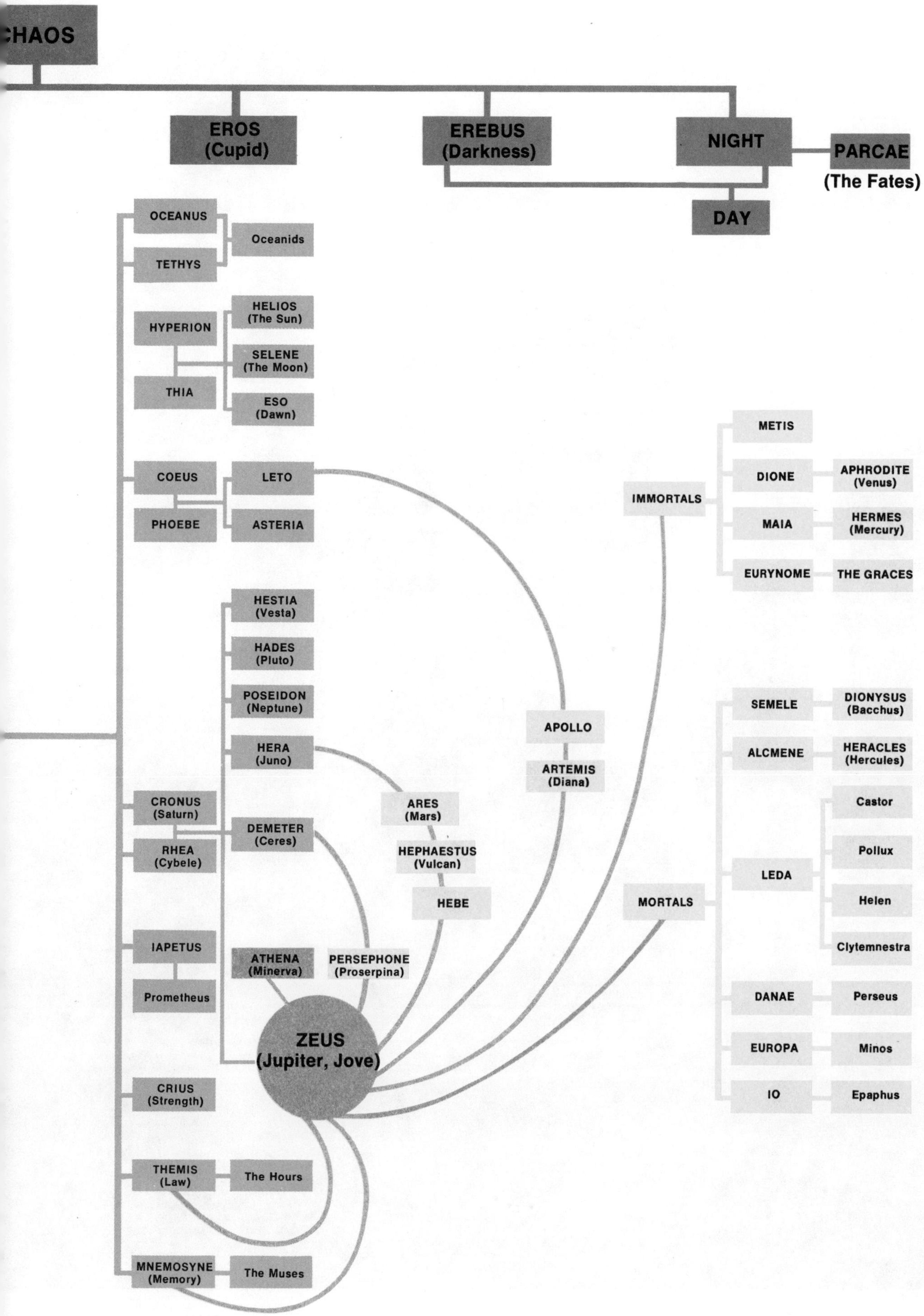

CHAOS

EROS
(Cupid)

EREBUS
(Darkness)

NIGHT

PARCAE
(The Fates)

DAY

OCEANUS

TETHYS

Oceanids

HYPERION

HELIOS
(The Sun)

SELENE
(The Moon)

THIA

ESO
(Dawn)

COEUS

LETO

PHOEBE

ASTERIA

METIS

DIONE

APHRODITE
(Venus)

MAIA

HERMES
(Mercury)

EURYNOME

THE GRACES

IMMORTALS

HESTIA
(Vesta)

HADES
(Pluto)

POSEIDON
(Neptune)

HERA
(Juno)

APOLLO

ARTEMIS
(Diana)

CRONUS
(Saturn)

RHEA
(Cybele)

DEMETER
(Ceres)

ARES
(Mars)

HEPHAESTUS
(Vulcan)

HEBE

SEMELE

DIONYSUS
(Bacchus)

ALCMENE

HERACLES
(Hercules)

Castor

Pollux

LEDA

Helen

Clytemnestra

IAPETUS

Prometheus

ATHENA
(Minerva)

PERSEPHONE
(Proserpina)

MORTALS

DANAE

Perseus

EUROPA

Minos

ZEUS
(Jupiter, Jove)

IO

Epaphus

CRIUS
(Strength)

THEMIS
(Law)

The Hours

MNEMOSYNE
(Memory)

The Muses

67

THE TIMES OF THE TIMELESS HEROES

At first the stories of the mythical Greek heroes were handed down by word of mouth from one generation to the next. Later they were collected by wandering poet-minstrels, who sang or recited these story-songs from country to country, from kingdom to kingdom. In a way our folk singers today are doing the same thing with their songs in which they tell what is happening in the world.

Throughout the ages there have always been people who performed heroic deeds. Myths and legends grew up about these heroes. You'll find that many myths tell similar stories of heroes triumphing over enemies. One hero may remind you of another. In the last chapter we talked about Greek and Roman heroes, and now you're going to hear about two more heroes—Roland and El Cid. All these heroes had similar traits. They were people of courage who devoted their lives to causes they believed in. Their deeds, sung by troubadours, crossed the borders of their native lands and became part of the world's literature.

And now that we're coming to meet some new heroes, where shall I begin? Maybe I should start with the knight Roland. We don't know very much about

Roland, except that he was a real person. His real name was Hruolandos and he lived in the time of Charlemagne, the King of the Franks and the founder of the Holy Roman Empire.

Beginning in the year 1,000, the people of southern France made pilgrimages to the Church of Saint-Romain-de-Blaye. They believed that Roland's tomb had been placed in this church. Roland also became the main character of the greatest medieval French poem, the *Song of Roland*.

The poem tells of an actual historical event that took place in the year 778. In the poem many of the historical happenings were changed for one reason or another. Maybe the poet thought the changes improved the story and made it more exciting. But first let's look at the historical account.

THE AGE OF CHARLEMAGNE

We are in the age of Charlemagne (742?-814). Charlemagne, or Charles the Great, ruled over the Franks, a Germanic tribe that lived in what is today approximately France, the Netherlands, and Belgium. He wished to free Spain from the Moors, the conquerors of that country. Charlemagne led a huge army to Saragossa, a city in northern Spain. Just as he reached the gates of the city, his army was fiercely attacked by a strong force of Arab cavalry. After a savage battle, the King ordered his men to retreat. The Frankish army retreated through a pass in the Pyrenees mountains until they came to the village of Roncesvalles. When most of the army had gotten safely through the village, out of the surrounding brush suddenly appeared thousands of Basques who lived in the Pyrenees mountains. The Basques hated the Franks, and in the course of the battle, they killed the entire rear guard of the Frankish army. One of the slain officers was Count Hruolandos. And this is where the legend takes over.

ROLAND

In the *Song of Roland*, Count Hruolandos becomes Roland. We first come upon Roland in Imola, Italy, where his mother Berthe, Charlemagne's sister, and her husband had gone to take refuge from the King. The King was angry at them because they had married against his will. Later the couple and their child moved to Sutri, a small town near Rome. Here in this rural setting Roland grew into a strong and fearless young man. He did not know that his mother was a princess and that his father, a woodchopper, was a noble knight. Nor did he know that the emperor, Charlemagne, was his uncle.

In the meantime the Moors had moved a large army against Rome. The Pope appealed to Charlemagne for help. He marched into Italy with an army, attacked the Moors and defeated them. It was at this time that Charlemagne met his nephew Roland purely by chance. He was won over by the lad's strength and handsome appearance. He pardoned Roland's parents and allowed them to return to France, and to places of honor in his court.

Some years later Charlemagne again went to war against the Moors. Though Roland had not yet been made a knight, he was permitted to fight beside Charlemagne in the battle of Aspromonte. During the fight, a Moor knocked the famous sword Durendal from the King's hand.

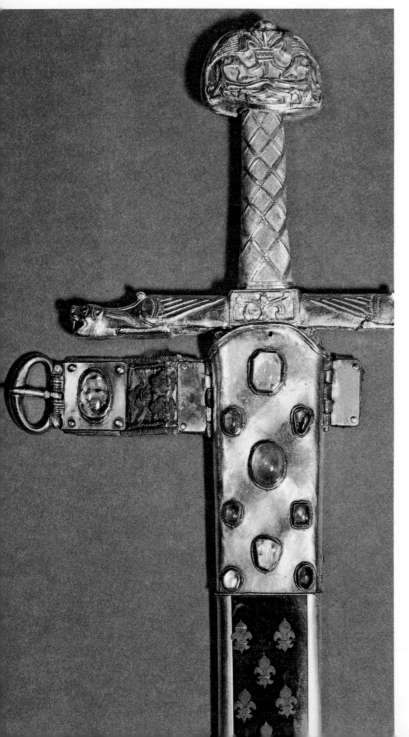

(Durendal was believed to be a magic sword that could never be broken.) Roland rushed to the King's side and saved his life by killing the Moor. In gratitude Charlemagne gave his sword to Roland and knighted him. The legend now introduces a new character, that of Oliver. The friendship between Roland and Oliver has become one of the most famous in world literature. But at first the two young men were enemies. Oliver was the nephew of Count Girard. The count held the city and the castle of Vienne and all the land about it, but he was unfriendly to Charlemagne. He rebelled against Charlemagne and after a fierce battle retreated with his men behind the city's walls.

Opposite page: Detail of the jewel-encrusted hilt of a sword believed to have been Charlemagne's.
Above: Roland draws his famous sword Durendal and battles with the enemy.
Left: The Castle of Este in northern Italy. According to legend, the young Roland played on the castle grounds.

After a long siege it was decided that the two nephews, Roland and Oliver, would fight each other. The entire war would be decided by the outcome of this fight. But after a long day's battle the contest ended in a tie. Roland and Oliver persuaded their uncles to make peace, and Oliver became one of the King's knights.

THE BATTLE OF RONCESVALLES

The *Song of Roland* sets the hero's last legendary adventure in the rugged Pyrenees mountains. After 7 years of fighting and conquering all of Spain except Saragossa, Charlemagne prepared to return to France with his army. However, he left a rear guard of 20,000 men under the command of Roland. Roland and the army were to protect the retreat of Charlemagne's men.

Above: A painting of one of the characters in Orlando Furioso (Wild Roland) *by Lodovico Ariosto.*
Opposite page: A painting showing the elegant costumes worn during the Age of Chivalry.

Before he left, the king gave Roland his hunting horn and said, "If you are in danger, blow the horn. I shall hear it wherever I am, and I shall come to your aid!"

Roland, his friend Oliver, and their army stationed themselves at the pass at Roncesvalles. Suddenly they found themselves attacked by an army of almost 100,000 Saracens. Defeat seemed certain. Oliver urged Roland to sound the horn and summon Charlemagne to their side. But Roland refused, for he was unwilling to put the King in unnecessary danger. He still hoped that he and his brave men could overcome the enemy.

The battle was a furious one, savagely fought. The Franks under Roland were beginning to win when reinforcements came to help the enemy. Greatly out-numbered, one Frank after another fell in the desperate struggle. When only a handful of survivors remained, Roland

The legendary deeds of the heroes found an outstanding interpreter in Paul Gustave Doré, famous 19th-century illustrator of Orlando Furioso. Throughout history myths and legends have served as subjects for many noted artists and illustrators.

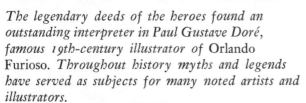

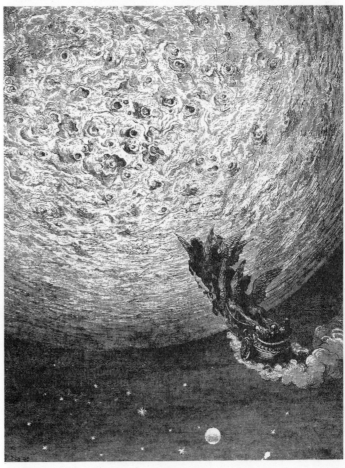

Above and left: Two paintings showing the death of the heroic Roland. Roland was the ideal knight. He was pure and fearless and faithful to his King. Even though he knew that it might mean his death, he refused to sound the call for help. He was unwilling to put the famous horn to his lips because he knew that this would place Charlemagne in grave danger.

Opposite page: An ivory hunting horn of the 11th century.

realized that there was no hope of victory. He decided to sound the horn to recall Charlemagne so that the king could avenge their defeat. He raised the horn to his lips and blew a great blast, hoping that Charlemange would hear him. The bloody battle continued and again Roland sounded the horn, this time weakly.

Charlemagne did hear the horn's cry for help and turned about to come to Roland's aid. The sound of the king's answering trumpets spread fear in the ranks of the Saracens and they fled from the battlefield. Roland was now alone; his dear and noble friend Oliver lay dead before him. Roland himself was mortally wounded. Gathering his last bit of strength, Roland tried to smash his magic sword Durendal against a rock. He did not want this sacred weapon to fall into

the hands of the enemy. The blade of the magic sword pierced the rock, but it would not break.

When Charlemagne came to the deserted battlefield and saw his noble warriors lying dead, he wept. He knelt at the side of his beloved Roland. And then in great fury he rose and pursued the fleeing enemy, killing many of them. The next day the King returned to France, where he buried Roland in the Church of Saint-Romain-de-Blaye. When Aude the Beautiful, Roland's beloved, heard of his death, she died of a broken heart. And so ends the *Song of Roland*.

EL CID, WARRIOR KNIGHT

A quick change of scene, boys and girls, and a new hero. One who is powerful, active, and fascinating. I introduce no less a man than Rodrigo Díaz de Vivar, an 11th-century nobleman. He is better-known as El Cid Campeador. Cid comes from the Arabic word *sidi*, which means "lord." Campeador means "champion." The legendary deeds of this knight from Castile are famous in literature. Down through the ages his action-filled life has inspired many poems and ballads, books and plays, an opera, and a moving picture.

Rodrigo, or Ruy, as he was called, took part in his first duel when he was just a youth. His old father had been insulted by a certain count. The old gentleman asked his three oldest sons to avenge him, but they could not. Ruy, the youngest son, demanded an apology from the count. He refused and Ruy challenged him to a duel. Ruy won the duel and the family's honor was avenged. For his courageous act, Ruy was taken to the court of King Ferdinand I and was brought up by the King's son Sancho.

ONE AGAINST FIVE

During the time of the Moorish invasion of Spain, news reached El Cid that five Moorish kings, each with an army, were attacking Spanish cities and villages. They had won many battles and were now sweeping over the land, taking riches and prisoners. El Cid quickly gathered an army of brave young men. It was a small army but it proved to be a good one. El Cid and his men rode into battle against the enemy. They fought valiantly and they won. The Moorish kings were made prisoners but later released to become servants of the victorious El Cid.

Some time later, Spain went through a period of much unrest and trouble. It seemed that King Ferdinand had made a will in which he divided the country among his three sons. To Sancho he left Castile; to Alfonso, León: and to García, Galicia.

You probably won't be surprised to hear that after their father's death the King's sons began fighting with one another for power. The ambitious Sancho attacked García, lost the battle, and was taken prisoner. El Cid, who was loyal to Sancho, came to his lord's defense and freed him. Sancho now turned against Alfonso and succeeded in taking over León.

El Cid's military talents were most useful to Sancho during the following years. However, Sancho was later assassinated and Alfonso returned to claim the thrones of Castile and León. Even though El Cid had earlier opposed Alfonso, El Cid remained at his court for nearly 10 years and even married his niece, Jimena. Later, Alfonso suspected El Cid of being disloyal and banished him from Castile.

But exile was not to be the end of El Cid's career by any means. He went to the Moorish kingdom of Saragossa, where

he served its kings for a number of years. He acted as a military leader and a political advisor. El Cid returned in triumph from his exile in Spain. He finally managed to capture Valencia, which he ruled until his death.

What a man El Cid was! Even after he fell into disfavor with the Spanish King, he continued to win fame, wealth, and position. He made no great contribution to Spanish history but he fired the imagination of many writers and poets.

Left: This is said to be the very sword El Cid used when he went into battle.

79

THE DARK AND ADVENTUROUS AGES

And now, boys and girls, let's get ready to leave again. Come along with me to the North, to the island of Great Britain. Here, centuries ago, the myths of the ancient Celtic people mingled with the religious and moral ideals of Christianity to create one of the most enduring legends of all—that of King Arthur and his knights of the Round Table.

A question that is often asked is—Did King Arthur ever exist?

No one knows for sure. But it is believed that a military leader named Arthur, who may have lived during the first part of the 6th century, became a hero to the Celts by defeating the Saxons who had invaded Britain.

The legend of Arthur grew over the centuries. Poets and storytellers in Britain, France, Germany, and other countries of Europe added their own versions to the story. The result is a legend that is a mixture of different ages and different cultures.

The story I am about to tell you is itself a retelling of the different accounts of King Arthur. Like many myths and legends, it begins with magic.

Once upon a time, the Devil, up to his usual mischief, decided to send an evil spirit to earth. He ordered it to marry an innocent young maiden and to abandon her as soon as a child was born. The evil spirit foolishly (as we shall see) chose a very religious young woman. Then he disappeared as soon as a son was born.

The girl, left all alone, asked a priest for help. The priest had the child baptized. The mother then retired to a convent where she devoted herself to prayer.

This is the origin of Merlin, who, because he was the son of a magical spirit, became himself a great magician. But since he was also the child of a pious woman, he could not be evil. To quote an old proverb: The Devil had made the pot but had forgotten the cover.

One of Merlin's exploits was the creation of the Round Table. And this is where Arthur enters the story.

KING ARTHUR

What's in a name? Some say that a name has nothing to do with the character and destiny of the one who carries it. Well, I'll let you judge for yourself. The name Arthur comes from a word that means Great Bear, and our Arthur grew up wild as a young bear.

He was the son of King Uther Pendragon. But he was raised first by the

81

magician Merlin and then by a knight, Sir Ector.

When King Uther died, all the great nobles met at the cathedral to choose a new king. Great was their astonishment when they arrived to see an immense stone in which a sword was stuck. (Some accounts say the sword was inserted into a blacksmith's anvil.) Written on the sword were words stating that whoever could remove it would be the true king of Britain. All the nobles tried but failed the test.

At this time Arthur, then just 15 years

The location of King Arthur's kingdom, Camelot, is unknown. But the court and the famous Round Table might have been located in a castle like this one in Scotland.

old, was hurrying to fetch a sword for his foster brother, Sir Kay. Seeing the sword in the stone, he grasped it by the hilt and effortlessly lifted it out. To convince the doubting nobles, he replaced the sword and again withdrew it from the stone.

Young Arthur was proclaimed king and set up his court in a kingdom called Camelot. Just where Camelot was, though, no one today knows. The Round Table established by Merlin stood for the equality of the knights who sat at it. One seat, however, was left vacant. It was reserved for a very special knight, one whose appearance would signal the beginning of a new era.

Arthur married the princess Guinevere. At the wedding banquet all the knights of the Round Table swore an oath to aid each other and to devote their weapons and strength to defend people who needed their protection.

After Merlin had completed his work, he fell under the spell of an enchantress named Vivian, who was known as the Lady of the Lake. He lived with her as a prisoner in an invisible castle in the midst of an enchanted lake.

LANCELOT OF THE LAKE

Meanwhile, across the sea in Brittany, a region of northwestern France, the noble King Ban was at war with a rival king. Ban fought courageously but was forced to flee with his queen and young son, Lancelot. He was on his way to seek

The legend of King Arthur and his knights of the Round Table is a combination of early Celtic myth and poems and chronicles of the Middle Ages. According to the legend, whoever could remove the sword stuck in an anvil (or stone) would become king of Britain. Many knights and nobles tried without success, until a boy effortlessly removed the sword. This boy, Arthur, whose teacher was the magician Merlin, became king.

aid from King Arthur when he died. While his queen wept over his body, the figure of a woman appeared, took the infant Lancelot, and disappeared with him into the waters of a lake.

The mysterious woman was none other than Vivian, the Lady of the Lake. She brought Lancelot to her castle and raised him with great care. On reaching the age of 18, he was taken to King Arthur by Vivian who asked the King to knight him and take him into his service.

And so Lancelot became a member of the Round Table. In fact, he became the greatest of all the knights of King Arthur. Lancelot met Queen Guinevere and, captivated by her beauty, fell in love with her. He swore never to love another woman. Lancelot had a chance to prove his devotion when the Queen was kidnapped by a knight named Sir Meliagrance. On the way to rescue her, Lancelot had the adventure of the cart.

A short time after setting out he was attacked by archers belonging to Meliagrance's company. Their arrows killed his horse and Lancelot found himself helpless, weighted down as he was by his heavy armor. Seeing a cart, he asked the

driver to carry him on his journey.

Now in those days such a cart was used to carry condemned criminals to their place of execution, and Lancelot was forced to listen to the jeers of the people as he rode along. But he continued on his mission and after many hazardous adventures rescued Queen Guinevere and brought her safely back to Camelot.

GALAHAD AND PERCIVAL

One day Lancelot came to the castle of King Pelles, who had a daughter named Elaine. The King wished Elaine to marry Lancelot for he had been told that they would have a son destined to discover the Holy Grail. This was the cup that Christ was believed to have drunk from at the Last Supper. It was to become the great quest for the knights of the Round Table.

But since Lancelot loved Queen Guinevere and would never willingly marry anyone else, the king cast a spell on him. Under its influence Lancelot married Elaine. When he awoke and realized that he had been tricked, he left her, vowing

These medieval illustrations show various scenes from the legend of King Arthur.

Opposite page: The Round Table, with the vacant seat reserved for the purest knight.

Above, top and bottom: Two views of the Holy Grail.

Above, right: Lancelot and the other knights vow to search for the sacred cup.

never to see her again. When their son was born, Elaine named him Galahad.

Meanwhile, in a distant castle, another young man was growing up. His name was Percival, or Parsifal in German legend. Because his father and two brothers had been killed in battle, Percival's mother swore to keep him far from battle and knightly deeds. She raised him as a simple country lad. But one day when he saw some knights, he knew at once that he wanted to be one of them. He made his way to King Arthur's court. At first he was laughed at because of his country dress and manner. But when Percival made a young maiden smile who had never smiled before, he was led to a seat at the Round Table and made welcome.

Sometime later another young man arrived at King Arthur's court, escorted by an old hermit. Lancelot at once recognized him as his son, Galahad. The hermit led the young knight to the chair that had long remained empty. He lifted a cover from it and showed that on it was written Galahad's name. It was the chair reserved for the purest of all the knights of the Round Table.

THE SEARCH FOR
THE HOLY GRAIL

One day a vision of the Holy Grail appeared to the members of the Round Table. Then all the knights took leave of Arthur and left to search for the sacred cup.

The knights searched long and far and had many adventures. Some were never to return from their dangerous quest.

The first to catch a glimpse of the holy cup was Sir Lancelot. In a castle, in the center of a large table covered by a scarlet velvet cloth, the sacred cup appeared to

him as in a dream. But he was not permitted to see more, for he had given up divine love for the love of Guinevere.

Galahad and Percival had many adventures searching for the Grail. Later they were joined by Sir Bohort, Lancelot's cousin. The three knights reached the castle where the cup was kept. At a sign, the velvet covering fell away revealing the shining, sacred Grail. Galahad, Percival, and Bohort then set sail for the Holy Land to restore the cup to its original home. There Galahad was chosen king and there he stayed until he died. At his death he remained clutching the Holy Grail in his hand.

Percival entered a monastery, while Bohort returned to King Arthur to tell of the marvelous adventure and the successful quest.

THE DEATH OF ARTHUR

And now, I must end the tale of King Arthur and his knights. It is a sad end, for it deals with the death of the noble Arthur and the destruction of the Round Table.

A revolt led by Sir Modred, King Arthur's nephew, led to a great battle of all the knights. Arthur was mortally wounded in the battle. As he lay dying, he told the faithful Sir Bedivere to take his miraculous sword, Excalibur, and throw it into the lake. Reluctant to lose such a magnificent weapon, Bedivere hesitated, but finally at the King's insistence, he hurled the sword far into the lake. A hand shot up from the water, grasped the blade, and then disappeared into the lake. Hearing this, Arthur knew that the sword had returned to its owner—the Lady of the Lake. Then three maidens came to carry Arthur off to the island of Avalon.

The legend of Percival, or Parsifal, has inspired poets and musicians. The 19th-century German composer Richard Wagner wrote an opera called Parsifal. *The illustration above is from the first act. Parsifal is a symbol of the purity of the spirit and the ideal of chivalry, the knightly code.*

SONG OF THE NORTH

Now, stay very close to me, boys and girls. We're about to enter the dark forests on the banks of the Rhine River. We're going to explore the fascinating, mysterious world of German and Norse mythology.

Quick! Look down there, among those ancient, twisted oaks. Do you see those little lights moving around the tree trunks? No, they're not fireflies, they're elves, and one of their favorite pastimes is dancing. Sometimes they've been known to dance all night long, and if we look real hard, in the morning we can see the marks called a magic ring, left in the grass by their tiny feet.

But let's not get too close; the elves might not like it. I've heard strange talk of people disappearing after they've broken the elves' circle, and it's even said that these naughty spirits can make you have bad dreams at night. Let's get out of here before anything like that happens to us!

I can hear girls' voices singing over there on the riverbanks. That's the chorus of the ondines, graceful water sprites who may help people by telling their fortunes, but who sometimes drag men down to the river bottom, never to be seen again.

The loveliest voice of all comes from the rock where the maiden called Lorelei sings. Her fascinating song makes sailors forget the dangers of this part of the Rhine, and many of their boats have been wrecked here. It is said that this is Lorelei's revenge, for she was betrayed by a handsome young fisherman whom she loved.

But what's happening now? The moon has disappeared. Those dark clouds must be the Valkyries, warrior maidens who carry the souls of heroes slain in battle to Valhalla—home of the gods in German and Norse mythology. There they will live until the last battle, against the gods of the underworld, led by the terrible Loki. And after that fearful, fiery day, there will be no more earth, no more men, and no more gods. It will be the dark time known as the Twilight of the Gods.

ODIN

For a minute there I really thought the last battle was about to begin. But then I pinched myself, and here I am, back with you, boys and girls. I'm sure you're impatient to hear the rest of my tale. (It's a good thing I'm not Uncle Scrooge—

he'll even stop a conversation in the middle, just to save breath!)

German and Norse mythology comes down to us from thousands of years ago, when various Germanic tribes wandered across northern Europe, from Scandinavia to the plains around the Rhine. Many of these myths were first set down—some in prose and some in poetry—about A.D. 1000 in an Icelandic book called the *Edda*.

The *Edda* tells of the origin of the gods and the world. The gods are grouped into two families—the Aesir and the Vanir—along with the Valkyries, elves, and other creatures like those I told you about.

The leader of all the gods was Odin, god of war and poetry and the creator of man. Odin was so wise that he knew all the magic formulas—those that cured illness, defeated enemies, and those for love.

Above: The last rays of the setting sun reflect in the waters of the Rhine. This river touches six European countries on its way to the sea. Many legends are associated with the Rhine. Among the most poetic is the story of Lorelei, a young girl who drowned herself after her sweetheart deserted her. She was transformed into a water spirit who sang so beautifully that sailors were drawn ever closer, until their ships were wrecked on the rocks. Below: The rock where Lorelei is said to sing is located below the German town of Sankt Goarshausen.

Opposite page: Pfalz Castle, near Kaub, Germany, is one of many along the Rhine. Built on a reef in the river, it dates from the 14th century.

And he knew how to read the runes—mysterious symbols carved on stones and tree trunks.

But Odin did not gain his great knowledge easily. In fact, he had to pay a terrible price for it. Let me tell you how it happened.

In the underworld, among the roots of the giant ash tree called Yggdrasil, was the fountain of wisdom. It was guarded by a powerful demon, or evil spirit, named Mimir. Odin knew that in order to be a wise leader, he had to drink from the fountain. But when he descended to the underworld, Mimir struck a hard bargain. He demanded one of Odin's eyes in exchange for allowing him to drink.

That is why Odin is usually shown wearing a helmet that hides half of his face. He is often described as a tall, powerful man with a long beard, accom-

Above and opposite page: Sketches for stage sets for Richard Wagner's opera The Rhinegold. *The opera is the first of Wagner's four works known as* The Ring of the Nibelung, *based on themes from German and Norse mythology.*

94

panied by two crows and two wolves. He was able to gallop through the sky faster than the wind on his wonderful eight-footed stallion, Sleipnir.

THOR

Odin's wife, Frigga, was a fertility goddess. She blessed the earth, so that crops would flourish, and she blessed marriages, so that humans would have many children.

Odin and Frigga had two sons, the gods Balder and Thor. Balder was handsome, wise, and kind, but he was destined to die young, thanks to the evil Loki. (I'll tell you about that terrible character in a little while, boys and girls.)

Thor, on the other hand, was very tall and strong, absolutely fearless, and had a deep, booming voice exactly right for the god of thunder and lightning. His weapon was an enormous hammer named Mjolnir, which he could throw with great accuracy. Once Mjolnir had hit its target, it returned to Thor's iron-gloved hand, just like a boomerang!

Thor traveled in a chariot drawn by two goats. Often, to satisfy his huge appetite, he would kill and roast the goats. When he wanted to continue on his way, he would touch the goatskins with his hammer, and the goats would come back to life.

But Thor had his enemies, too, such as the giants. Once they even stole his hammer, leaving him almost defenseless. The giants' leader would not give it back unless he were allowed to marry Freya, the lovely goddess of beauty. By a trick, Thor posed as Freya, and when he had the hammer back, he slew all the giants.

LOKI

The evil god Loki was as sly as a fox and as crafty as a snake. And he could turn himself into either of these animals, or any others, in an instant by using his great magical powers.

He sometimes advised the other gods or used his powers to help them. But generally he used his cleverness for evil. When he was young, his tricks were merely mischievous, designed only to annoy their victims. But as he grew older, Loki's true nature took over, and he came to enjoy tormenting the other gods. He grew more and more jealous of the great Odin, though they had once sworn a vow of friendship.

Loki's cruelty sometimes had far-reaching consequences. For example, once he killed one of the three sons of the dwarf Hreidmar, and then. . . . And then nothing, for the moment, boys and girls. Before we go any further, I'd like to take a moment to introduce a famous legend.

Way back in the beginning of the world, the god Odin, with the help of the other Aesirs, had to fight a battle against the giants of the underworld, led by Ymir. Odin's forces won the battle, and Odin used Ymir's body to form the earth; his blood to form the sea; his bones, the mountains; his hair, the trees; his skull, the sky; and his brain, the clouds. And the dwarfs were born of Ymir's flesh. Now they ruled the underworld and its treasures. And they were called the Nibelungs.

Siegfried's daring rescue of Brünnhilde from the ring of fire is one of the highlights of Richard Wagner's opera Siegfried.
Above and opposite page: Two pages from a set designer's sketchbook for a production of the opera.

97

THE RING OF
THE NIBELUNG

The dwarf Andvari, king of the Nibelungs, was guardian of the magic golden treasure of the sea. He knew that whoever possessed the gold and a magic ring would obtain endless riches and power.

There are dozens of versions of this legend, which was first told in the *Edda*. In the 13th century, a German poet used the legend, with variations of his own, to write *The Song of the Nibelungs*. And in the 19th century, the great German composer Richard Wagner selected the most dramatic parts of the legend and added others. The four operas he wrote on this theme form one of our greatest art treasures. *Das Rheingold* (*The Rhinegold*), *Die Walküre* (*The Valkyries*), *Siegfried*, and *Die Götterdämmerung*

(*The Twilight of the Gods*) are known throughout the world as *The Ring of the Nibelung*.

I'm sure you see that this legend has had such a long history and has undergone so many changes that it really can be most confusing. There are characters whose names change, characters who are killed and return to life, and so on.

Well, boys and girls, I'll try to put it all in some kind of order for you, leaving out most of the gory details. You see, the characters in the legend were very direct when they wanted to "get rid" of someone, whether it was an enemy or even a relative. Can you imagine what they did to strangers?!

Do you remember a while ago I started to tell you about the time when Loki killed one of the three sons of the dwarf Hreidmar? Let's pick up our story there.

In payment for his crime, Loki gave

Above and opposite page: Two designs for a production of Siegfried. The hero is the last of the Volsungs, a powerful family favored by the god Odin. But they are finally overtaken by tragedy because of the curse on the Rhinegold.

Hreidmar the gold of the sea, which he had stolen, along with the magic ring, from Andvari. Andvari put a curse on the gold, so that it would bring ruin and death to all those who possessed it.

The curse soon took effect. Hreidmar's other two sons, Regin and Fafnir, demanded that their father share the gold with them. When he refused, Fafnir murdered him and drove his brother away, for he wanted to keep all of the gold himself. Finally, to make certain no one could steal it from him, he changed himself into a horrible dragon!

And now let me tell you about a character who's going to play an important part in the story.

SIGURD

According to one version of the legend, Sigmund, the head of a powerful family favored by the gods, is killed in battle. His wife is pregnant, and when the child is born, she names him Sigurd.

As a young man, Sigurd is educated by a tutor who is actually the dwarf Regin, still seeking revenge on his brother Fafnir in the hope of gaining the golden treasure for himself.

When Regin saw that Sigurd had grown into a brave, strong warrior and expert swordsman, he decided to use the young man in order to achieve his goal. The crafty dwarf rejoined the broken pieces of a magical sword that had been given to Sigurd's father by Odin.

Regin gave the now perfect sword to Sigurd and urged him to try it out by killing the dragon Fafnir. (Of course, he was careful not to mention that the dragon was his brother!) He also prom-

Two scenes from The Twilight of the Gods, *as seen by the great stage designer Nikolai Benois. In Norse mythology, the twilight of the gods usually meant the end of the world. Before a new and better world could be born, the old one had to be destroyed.*

ised that they would share the dragon's treasure between them.

Sigurd loved fighting and hunting, so he willingly accepted Regin's suggestion and set out on the dangerous task. He dug a deep pit and hid in it, waiting for the dragon to pass by. When Fafnir flew overhead, Sigurd was able to kill him with one blow of the magical sword.

Then Sigurd cut out the dragon's heart and roasted it, as Regin had told him to do. When he burned his fingers trying to see if it was done, he put them in his mouth to ease the pain. That is how,

through the magical powers of the dragon's blood, Sigurd suddenly found himself able to understand the language of the birds. He learned that the wicked Regin was planning to kill him and keep the gold for himself. He also learned from the birds that if he bathed in the dragon's blood, he would become invulnerable, which meant that no one would be able to harm him.

Sigurd covered himself from head to toe with the dragon's blood, but he did not notice that a tiny leaf had fallen onto one shoulder. And, of course, that single spot was not touched by the dragon's blood and did not become invulnerable. (What happens to Sigurd later because of this is part of another story.)

Sigurd finally killed Regin, took the gold and the ring, and set out to seek adventure.

THE RING OF FIRE

Sigurd rode and rode for many miles. One day he drew near a towering mountain. From its peak, bright flames leaped toward the sky. Behind that fearful, fiery curtain was a ring of shields, and in the center of the ring, a warrior dressed in armor lay sleeping on the ground.

Sigurd climbed the mountain and dared to ride through the flames. But when he knelt beside the sleeping warrior and removed his helmet, he suddenly saw that it was not a warrior at all, but a beautiful young girl.

The girl awoke by magic and told Sigurd that she was the Valkyrie Brynhild. Because she had disobeyed Odin, the powerful god condemned her to sleep inside the ring of fire. Only a hero courageous enough to brave the flames could free her. She and her rescuer would fall deeply in love, and because of this love Brynhild would become a mortal woman instead of a Valkyrie.

In the *Edda*, the legend ends with the marriage of Sigurd and Brynhild. But in *The Song of the Nibelungs*, things happen differently. Sigurd is called Siegfried, Brynhild is Brünnhilde, and the story is set in the royal court of Burgundy. Because of a magic potion, Siegfried forgets Brünnhilde and marries the Princess Kriemhild. By using a trick, he persuades Brünnhilde to marry the king's son. When Brünnhilde discovers that she has been betrayed, she has Siegfried killed and then commits suicide. The king's adviser Hagen takes the treasure of the Nibelungs and hides it at the bottom of the Rhine.

And so the happy ending in the *Edda* became a tragedy in later versions. And what happened to the treasure? Well, boys and girls, it is still in the Rhine, waiting for someone brave enough to ignore the ancient curse and look for it!

THE FLYING DUTCHMAN

Speaking of curses, I'm taking along all my good luck charms on the rest of our journey. Not that I'm superstitious, but you never know what might happen! Also, I'm not going to miss this chance to tell you about an old sea legend that still fascinates many people today.

One well-known form of the story concerns a sea captain named Vanderdecken, who was always boasting that he had no reverence for God and no fear of the Devil. For this, he was condemned to sail until Judgment Day around the Cape of Good Hope. He was never permitted to stop or drop anchor.

In the old days of seafaring, many sailors claimed to have seen the battered ship with its torn sails, riding on an ocean of

Part of a design for a stage set for Wagner's opera, The Flying Dutchman. *The scene was painted by Peter Bisseger for a production at Milan's great La Scala opera house.*

Above: Another stage set for The Flying Dutchman, *as presented at La Scala in Milan. The theme of this opera is not part of Norse or German mythology, but it belongs to Germany's great heritage of legends. Most of Richard Wagner's music was inspired by German myths and legends.*

clouds. The appearance of the Dutchman and his ship always meant bad luck.

As with most legends, there are several versions of this one. It has also been used as the theme for books, plays, and operas. Among these, the best-known is *Der Fliegende Holländer* (*The Flying Dutchman*), by the same Richard Wagner we discussed before.

In another version of this ghostly tale, the captain is called Von Falkenberg. He is condemned to drift forever on the North Sea in a ship without a helm. To pass the time, he plays dice with the Devil for his soul.

And now that we've reached northern waters, let's forget about ghosts and curses and make our last stop in the Land of Heroes.

THE LAND OF HEROES

Here we are in Finland, boys and girls —that beautiful and somewhat mysterious land of northern Europe. We're sure to find a wealth of poetic legends and myths to explore here.

Most of Finland's ancient folktales and ballads were handed down from generation to generation by bards (traveling poet-singers). These stories and songs were first collected in the early 19th century by a Finnish doctor and university professor named Elias Lönnrot. He spent many years going from village to village, listening to the old tales and poems, and selecting the best versions. In 1835 he first published them as the *Kalevala*, and the poem soon became the country's national epic. Its publication date is still celebrated as a holiday in Finland today.

"Kalevala" is the poetic name for Finland. It means "land of heroes," and it stands for the homeland of the ancient, godlike characters called the Sons of Kaleva.

In the final version of the *Kalevala*, published in 1849, there are 50 cantos (a canto is a division of a longer poem). They draw a picture of an imaginary world, inhabited by gods and men as well as magicians, witches, and fairies. The chief figure among all of these is the wise Väinamöinen, who is a kind of spiritual leader. He can predict the future and is also the finest singer in the world. His songs are usually accompanied by the playing of the *kantele*, a five-stringed harplike instrument that he invented.

Another character in the poem is the expert blacksmith called Ilmarinen. In the long-ago, misty days when the world was created, Ilmarinen was given the task of forging "the roof of the world."

Then there is the charming, carefree Lemminkäinen—a brave warrior who is considered a great "ladies' man." And we mustn't forget the powerful, tragic figure of Kullervo, destined to spend his life serving others.

The main theme of the poem is the conflict between Kalevala and the evil influence of the land of Pohjola, to the north.

Väinamöinen is the first of the three leading characters in the *Kalevala* to travel to Pohjola in search of a bride. When he arrives there, Louhi, the queen of Pohjola, promises him her own daughter's hand in marriage if he can forge the *sampo*. (The *sampo* is a mysterious object that will bring great power and wealth to anyone who possesses it. Does that sound familiar to you, boys and girls? You're right! It's quite similar to the ring of the Nibelungs, which we left many miles behind us to the south.)

When Väinamöinen asks Ilmarinen to perform this feat for him, Queen Louhi's daughter falls in love with the blacksmith instead. Väinamöinen steps aside and allows them to be married.

The tale doesn't end there, however, for the hot-tempered Lemminkäinen has somehow not been invited to the wedding. To avenge this insult, he decides to attack the land of Pohjola. But after he kills a great chieftain, Queen Louhi uses her magical powers and the people turn on him and drive him out.

Later on in the poem, Väinamöinen, Ilmarinen, and Lemminkäinen decide to return to Pohjola to get the *sampo*, so that it may bring prosperity to Kalevala. By playing sweet music on the *kantele*, they are able to lull the people of Pohjola to sleep and steal the precious object.

Just as they set sail, happy at their successful getaway, Lemminkäinen carelessly breaks into song and awakens the sleeping Pohjolans. When Queen Louhi discovers what has happened, she sends terrible winds and waves to batter their ship. They are able to ride out the storm, though the *sampo* is broken into tiny pieces. But even its fragments are powerful enough to insure good fortune for Kalevala, so the three heroes have succeeded in their quest.

The Queen of Pohjola never forgives the three for the theft of the *sampo*. In her fury, she uses all her magic against the land of Kalevala and its people. She sends cold and ice to freeze the earth and the sea, and once she even tries to prevent day and night from happening by imprisoning the sun and the moon. But Väinamöinen's wisdom and the power of the *sampo* are enough to defeat all of Queen Louhi's attempts to crush Kalevala. The Land of Heroes is able to stand against Pohjola.

When Väinamöinen sees that Pohjola and the forces of evil are no longer a threat, he decides his homeland can endure

Finland is also known as the Land of Heroes.

Opposite page, top: Lapland may be the Pohjola of Finnish mythology. Middle: The 15th-century castle of Olavinlinna once guarded Finland's eastern border. Bottom: A chain of sparkling lakes is one of the beauties of the Finnish countryside.

Right: The sea has cut deep, fiordlike bays into Finland's coastline.

without his leadership. He sails away forever and the main story of the *Kalevala* ends.

Like many other myths and legends, those of the *Kalevala* inspired artists, writers, and composers. In the 19th century the Finnish novelist and playwright Aleksis Kivi published several works based on it. Later, the painter Aksel Gallén-Kallela produced a large number of scenes illustrating events and characters from the pages of the poem.

But the stories of the *Kalevala* were most important of all to Finland's greatest composer, Jean Sibelius. In such works as *Kullervo*, the *Lemminkäinen Suite*, and *Pohjola's Daughter*, he expressed through music what the *Kalevala* said in words.

If I had the magical *sampo* right now, I'd wish us out of the chilly north so that we could take a look at the myths of a warmer climate. Let's do it anyway!

This scene was painted by Aksel Gallén-Kallela, one of Finland's best-known artists. Gallén-Kallela based many of his works on events from the Finnish epic poem, the Kalevala. *The painting is in the National Gallery in Helsinki.*

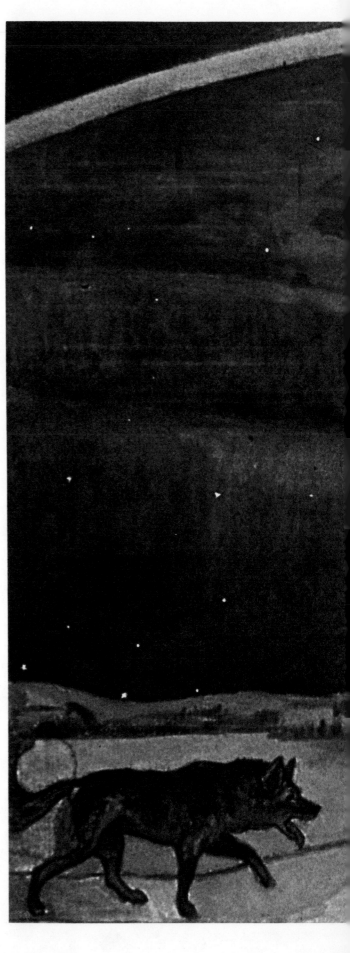

IN THE LAND OF THE PLUMED SERPENT

My friends, I want you to know I have just taken a cram course in untongue-tying. I took it to help me pronounce some of the words we will find in this chapter on Mexican Indian myths and legends. Your old friend Minnie has run the risk of dislocating her jaw several times trying to pronounce words like "Huitzilopochtli," "Tenochtitlán," and "Quetzalcoatl." I wouldn't like to see that happen to you. So I have boned up on pronunciation before acting as your guide through these jaw-breaking legends!

I am sure you boys and girls know that long ago, before the Spaniards came, the Indians of Mexico had great cities and a very advanced way of life. They also had a complicated religion, with many gods and stories about these gods. When the Spaniards came from over the sea, they did not come as friendly tourists. They came as conquerors with guns, which the Indians had never seen. They destroyed the cities, made slaves of the Indians, and stamped out their religion. But the stories about the gods lived on. The most famous legend, about the god Quetzalcoatl, the

The Aztec calendar stone, with the face of the sun god Tonatiuh in the center.

Plumed Serpent, helped make it easy for the Spaniard Hernando Cortes to conquer Mexico. It was the worst case of mistaken identity of all time, and if you'll stay with me on our journey south of the border, you'll hear about it very soon.

Quetzalcoatl was the god of the Toltecs, great builders who lived in the Valley of Mexico before the Aztecs came. But Quetzalcoatl was not just a tribal god. Word of his goodness and his knowledge of arts, crafts, and sciences spread, and he was a figure in myths all over Mexico. He was a white god, tall and strong with a thick beard, who had appeared from over the sea. He brought a golden age to Tula, the Toltec capital.

In time the gods of the neighboring peoples became envious of Quetzalcoatl and decided to humiliate him. They asked him to a feast in the public square of Tula and got him drunk on a popular drink called pulque. The next day Quetzalcoatl felt so ashamed he resolved to leave Tula and the Toltecs forever. He journeyed eastward toward the sea. Several versions of what happened next are told. In one story he built a funeral pyre near the coast, threw himself on it, and rose from his own ashes as the morning star. In

111

another, when he reached the sea he sailed away on a raft of snakes. But all the stories said he would return later, in the year called Ce-Acatl. Well, boys and girls, what do you suppose happened in that year? Remember, a white god was expected, with a beard! But I'm getting ahead of my story!

In time the Toltec civilization declined, and the Aztecs became rulers of the Valley of Mexico. The Aztecs worshiped the war god, Huitzilopochtli. He had led

them from the place of seven caves in the northwest into the Valley of Mexico. He told them to move on until they saw an eagle sitting on a cactus holding a serpent in its beak. There, the god told them, they must found their city. One day the Aztecs' enemies drove them into swampy Lake Texcoco. Far in the swamp they took refuge on an island. And there, sitting on a cactus, was the eagle with the serpent in its beak! Here the Aztecs built Tenochtitlán, their great city, the forerunner of Mexico City.

By the late 1400's Tenochtitlán was a big and beautiful city of over 100,000 people, with 40 temples to Huitzilopochtli and the lesser gods. All went well until 1519, the year in the Aztec calendar when the god Quetzalcoatl was expected. When a white bearded traveler from across the sea arrived, the Aztec ruler Montezuma greeted him as Quetzalcoatl, the returning god. But, as you have already guessed, he wasn't Quetzalcoatl at all. He was Hernando Cortes, the Spanish conqueror. And within a few short years, he and his men destroyed Tenochtitlán, Montezuma, and the whole great civilization of the Aztecs.

Opposite page: A two-headed serpent made by the Aztecs in the 15th century, when their culture was at its height. The figure is inlaid with turquoise and mother-of-pearl. Above, left: A 12th-century Toltec statue found in Tula, the Toltec capital. This statue is a telamon, which means it was part of a supporting column for a building. Above, right: A carved wooden image of Tlaloc, the Aztec rain god, inlaid with turquoise and other stones. The Aztecs believed that Tlaloc made the earth fertile.

113

THE LEGENDS OF THE RAINBOW

Boys and girls, let's travel back to the time when our country was covered with tall forests and wide open plains. I can smell the perfume of the woods and prairies! Over there I see a rainbow! And here are my friends the elks, bears, coyotes, beavers, the streams, rivers, mountains—even the wind!

We are about to roam together through some legends of the forest and plains Indians. These legends are not like the ones I've told you about before. They did not grow out of a historical need but are the fruits of the imagination—the poetry of a people. Now off we go, boys and girls. We are going to travel on a sunbeam!

KUNYAN OF THE IROQUOIS

One day when the people of the Iroquois tribe were out tilling their fields, a strange shadow fell upon the land. All at once the sad wailing of a young girl reached their ears. The Iroquois were so upset they left their work and went to their chief for help.

"Please advise us," said an old Iroquois. "We were working away in the fields when we heard the cry of a young girl. But we could not find where the cry came from. Now we are afraid the cry may be a warning of disaster!"

At this point the chief's son Kunyan stepped forward. "I shall help you," he exclaimed. "I promise you, I shall find the answer to this puzzle."

Kunyan walked for many days and many nights. Finally he came to a cave. It was the den of the Northern Panther. Kunyan saw two jade eyes glowing in the dark. He felt an icy chill run down his spine. He heard the girl's cry, very near.

"Leave my kingdom or you shall die!" threatened the Panther. The young man made no answer. Suddenly the animal pawed the ground and a terrifying snake appeared. Kunyan threw himself on the snake and cut off its head with one blow of his hatchet. The Panther pawed the ground again and there appeared a ferocious beast. Kunyan shot an arrow into its heart and killed it. Then the Panther made ready to leap on Kunyan. And this time Kunyan killed the Panther with an arrow. From the dead body of the Panther came the voice of the young girl, saying "Thank you, Kunyan. You have

115

Opposite page and above: The Grand Canyon in winter and summer. On the floor of this most famous gorge of the Colorado River lives the Havasupai Indian tribe.

Right and opposite page: Plains Indians of North America, dressed in full costume. The braves are photographed in front of their tepees, the plains Indians' portable homes. Tepees are made of buffalo skins.

freed me from a terrible spell." Then she said, "Go back to your village. Just before you get there, you will see a small kernel of grain on the ground. I am that little kernel. Pick me up carefully."

Kunyan did as he was told. He found the kernel, planted it, and from that day on, the Iroquois knew how to grow grain!

FLYING HOOF

Flying Hoof was a little boy to whom Mother Nature had given a great talent for painting. The boy's real name was Nanuk, but he was called Flying Hoof because he had an elk calf for a friend.

Nanuk's favorite hobby was painting. By mixing different plants and squeezing out the juice, the boy was able to obtain wonderful colors. One day the wicked giant Nabaca saw Nanuk's beautiful paintings and decided to kidnap the little artist. The giant grabbed Nanuk and carried him off to his kingdom far away.

But the evil giant had not counted on the elk calf, who followed after them.

During the night Flying Hoof realized that he wasn't alone. "Don't cry, little brother," said the calf. "Wait till I grow up, and I will carry you home!"

The little elk grew bigger day by day, and one morning Flying Hoof saw before him a huge magnificent elk. "Quick, climb up on my back!" said the animal. "But first gather up some earth, a stone, and some moss."

The little boy did as his friend told him, and then the two raced together over the wide prairies. But the giant soon set out after them. Before long he sighted the boy and the elk.

Just then the elk told the boy to throw his fistful of earth over his shoulder. Flying Hoof obeyed. The fistful of earth hit the ground and became many hills, so many that they slowed the giant up. The elk and his friend then rested awhile, but soon the giant appeared again. The elk

Opposite page: A waterfall in Yellowstone National Park, in Wyoming. Plains Indians lived in this region before the white man came.

took up his race once more, telling the boy to drop the moss. The moss became swamps and huge puddles of quicksand, into which the giant immediately sank.

Then Flying Hoof threw the stone, and the earth trembled and shook frightfully. Black clouds filled the sky, and before Flying Hoof's amazed eyes rose immense mountains. This, according to one story, is how the Rocky Mountains were born.

We've come a long way together, haven't we, boys and girls? On the road we've met gods and goddesses, magicians and sorcerers, giants and centaurs. Just turn the corner, close your eyes, and dream a little. If you like, I am always here, your faithful Minnie, ready to take off with you again for the marvelous Land of Legend.

Herds of wild horses such as these once roamed over the Great Plains.

INDEX

124